THE
ENCYCLOPEDIA
OF
EMBROIDERY
TECHNIQUES

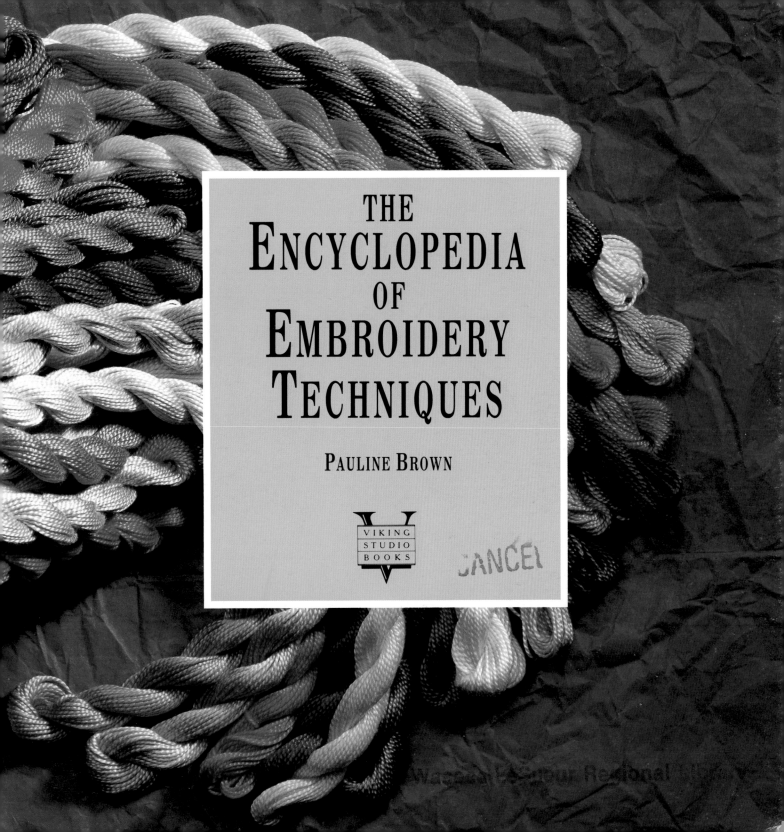

THE
ENCYCLOPEDIA
OF
EMBROIDERY
TECHNIQUES

PAULINE BROWN

VIKING
STUDIO
BOOKS

A QUARTO BOOK

VIKING STUDIO BOOKS
Published by the Penguin Group
Penguin Books USA Inc., 375 Hudson Street,
New York, New York 10014, U.S.A.

Penguin Books Ltd, 27 Wrights Lane,
London W8 5TZ, England
Penguin Books Australia Ltd, Ringwood, Victoria,
Australia
Penguin Books Canada Ltd, 2801 John Street,
Markham, Ontario, Canada L3R 1BR
Penguin Books (N.Z.) Ltd, 182–90 Wairau Road,
Auckland 10, New Zealand
Penguin Books Ltd, Registered Offices
Harmondsworth, Middlesex, England

First published by Viking Studio Books, an imprint
of Penguin Books USA, Inc.

First printing August, 1994
10 9 8 7 6 5 4 3 2 1

Library of Congress Catalog Card Numb

This book was designed and produced by
Quarto Inc., 6 Blundell Street,
London N7 9BH, United Kingdom

Senior art editor Amanda Bakhtiar
Designer Kathy Gummer
Illustrators Elsa Godfrey, Rob Shone
Embroidery samples Jane Dew of The Creative
Company
Photographers Sue Baker, Chas Wilder
Picture researcher Emma Enthoven
Senior editor Hazel Harrison
Copy editors Hazel Harrison, Michele Clark
Editorial director Sophie Collins
Art director Moira Clinch

Typeset by Genesis Typesetting, Rochester, Kent
Manufactured by Regent Publishing Services Ltd.,
Hong Kong
Printed in China

ISBN: 0-670-85568-5 (cloth); ISBN: 0 14 02.3771 2
(paperback)

CONTENTS

MAKING A START

Embroidery in the late 20th century has come a long way from the traditions of the past. However, the basic methods still hold good – without sound technique and suitable materials and equipment, embroiderers are unlikely to be able to exploit their ideas to create exciting and innovative work.

Most people manage with quite a small basic set of tools: scissors, pins and needles, tape measure and embroidery frame, and these, together with an iron and a sewing machine, are all that are needed to start.

Needles
It is essential to choose a needle which suits both the fabric and thread and the type of embroidery you are undertaking. The needle should pass easily through the fibers of the fabric, and the yarn through the eye of the needle. Needle size is designated by number, with the lowest number in each category signifying the longest and thickest.

Embroidery (or crewel) needles in sizes 1–10 have long eyes which will take embroidery floss, silks, and linens, and fine wools. They are suitable for a wide range of embroidery techniques.

Quilting needles, also known as "betweens," and made in sizes 1–10, are short with small, round eyes. They are ideal for making the quick, even stitching needed for techniques such as quilting and hemming with fine thread.

Chenille needles, in sizes 13–24, have sharp points and large eyes, and will take all types of thick yarn as well as ribbon and raffia.

Tapestry needles are similar to chenilles, and also come in sizes 13–24, but have blunt points which slip between the threads of canvas or the fibers of evenweave linen, making them the correct choice for needlepoint and all the counted thread methods.

Other specialist needles include long, fine *beading needles*, and *leather needles* whose triangular points will pierce all types of leather, suede, or plastic.

Bodkins are for threading elastic, ribbons, and cords, while *circular needles* are good for three-dimensional embroidery.

Threads
Good-quality thread and yarns are essential, and they should be selected not only for practical reasons, but also for esthetic ones: color and texture are both vital factors in embroidery.

There are so many different types of thread on the market

Circular
needles

Chenille needles

Darners

Bodkins

Tapestry needles

Embroidery or
crewel needles

Beading needles

Quilting
needles

Leather needles

Metallic
threads

Pearl
cotton

Tapestry yarns in 2-, 3-, 4-ply

today that the choice may at
first be overwhelming.
Indeed, anything which can
be threaded through the eye
of a needle can be put to use
in an imaginative way for
experimental work. Besides
conventional embroidery
threads, knitting and crochet
yarn, ribbons, and cords are
also readily available, while
some of the more specialist
items can be purchased by
mail order.

Cotton threads in a range of
colors and thicknesses are
widely used for all types of
embroidery, as they are hard-
wearing and washable.
Stranded floss is particularly
versatile because the six
strands can be divided to
produce a number of
thicknesses. This makes it
suitable for different effects
and techniques, particularly

for surface stitches. For
counted thread work,
changes of tone can be
achieved by varying the
number of strands. In
needlepoint, cotton can add
luster to contrast with the
matte texture of the more
usual woolen threads.

Pearl cotton (perlé) is a shiny,
twisted yarn which comes in
balls and skeins in three
thicknesses – 3, 5, and 8. It is
suitable for surface
embroidery and needlepoint,
as well as for coarser types of
counted thread work.

Coton à broder has a slight
sheen and is of fine twisted
construction. It is particularly
good for counted thread
techniques and smocking as
there are no strands to
separate.

Matte embroidery cotton is a
thick cotton yarn with a matte

surface; it can be used for
needlepoint and work on
coarsely woven fabrics.

Woolen embroidery yarn
comes in several qualities and
thicknesses. Although some
are primarily manufactured
for needlepoint, they are

7

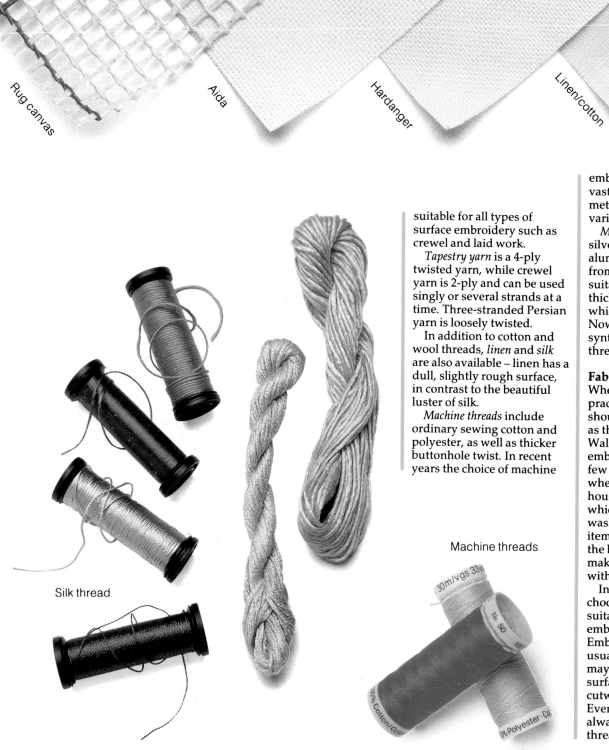

Rug canvas

Aida

Hardanger

Linen/cotton

Evenweave cotton

suitable for all types of surface embroidery such as crewel and laid work.

Tapestry yarn is a 4-ply twisted yarn, while crewel yarn is 2-ply and can be used singly or several strands at a time. Three-stranded Persian yarn is loosely twisted.

In addition to cotton and wool threads, *linen* and *silk* are also available – linen has a dull, slightly rough surface, in contrast to the beautiful luster of silk.

Machine threads include ordinary sewing cotton and polyester, as well as thicker buttonhole twist. In recent years the choice of machine

embroidery threads has been vastly extended to include metallic-finish and shaded varieties.

Metal threads come in gold, silver, copper, and aluminum, ranging in type from fine tambour threads suitable for stitching to thicker cords and braids which have to be couched. Nowadays many people use synthetic threads for metal-thread embroidery.

Fabrics

When choosing fabrics, the practical aspect of the project should be considered, as well as the color and texture. Wallhangings and embroidered panels present few practical barriers, whereas garments and household items need a fabric which can be cleaned or washed. For all decorative items, the texture and color of the background fabric will make a visual impact together with the other materials used.

In addition, it is essential to choose fabrics which are suitable for the particular embroidery technique. Embroidery fabrics are usually cotton or linen, which may be closely woven for surface embroidery and cutwork techniques. Evenweave fabrics, which are always used for counted thread work, are woven, with

Silk thread

Machine threads

between 10 and 32 threads per inch. Some, such as Aida and Hardanger fabrics, are constructed with a double-thread weave.

Dress and furnishing fabrics in both natural and synthetic fibers are available in a wide range of textures and patterns. These may be incorporated into appliqué projects or used as backgrounds.

For needlepoint embroidery, there are two main types of woven canvas, those with single or double threads. Both are available in various widths and gauges (or threads per inch). Single (or mono) canvas comes in gauges ranging from 10 to 24 threads per inch and is more adaptable for stitching a variety of stitches. Double (or Penelope) canvas is mainly used for tramming or for fine details. Rug canvas in gauges 3 to 7 is suitable for large-scale work, and plastic canvas, a recent innovation, is used for rigid articles such as boxes and placemats.

There are a number of subsidiary types of fabrics which are used by embroiderers to support or pad their work.

Batting is usually made of synthetic fibers, but is available in silk, wool, and cotton. Its main use is for quilting (page 101) or for padding and stuffing three-dimensional shapes. Felt can also act as a firm padding or as an insertion in types of appliqué.

Non-woven iron-on or sew-in interfacings used by dressmakers are also suitable for stiffening fabrics for appliqué or for backing finished wallhangings; bonding web is extremely useful for fusing fabrics together.

Dissolvable fabrics used for making lacy effects and constructions by machine come in either hot- or cold-water types (see pages 86–7).

Other equipment

Two pairs of sharp scissors are needed for embroidery – a large pair for cutting fabric and a small pair for trimming threads and cutting intricate pieces or holes.

Pinking shears are useful for cutting decorative edges. A stiletto, often found in old sewing boxes, is used for making eyelets in cutwork or eyelet lace.

Using a thimble is largely a matter of personal choice, but will prevent sore fingers when quilting or working in leather. A block of beeswax is useful for techniques such as quilting and metal thread embroidery. The thread is drawn through it, preventing it from becoming twisted and helping to give it strength.

Design materials

Most of the equipment needed for designing embroidery is readily at hand. A sketchbook, pencils, and some colored crayons or felt-tip pens are all that are needed for your initial attempts.

If you prefer to use paint, watercolor, poster, and gouache are the most useful. Different types of paper, including tracing and graph paper, are required for some methods, while colored and textured papers and cardboard are good for stencils or for trying out bold ideas. Paper scissors, a craft knife, and a metal ruler are useful implements when working with paper or cardboard. Fabric and paper adhesives, masking tape, and geometry instruments can all be purchased when the need arises.

Transferring designs

There are a number of ways of transferring and marking the design onto the background fabric. The method and the type of marker depend on the technique chosen, the fabric, and the intricacy of the design. In every case, the design should be very lightly marked so that it will not show when the embroidery is finished. Fabric markers include dressmakers' chalk and pencils, water-soluble and air-soluble pens, transfer and permanent pens.

Direct tracing is probably the simplest method for transparent materials. If the fabric is opaque, it can be taped to a window (or a light box) with the design below.

Dressmakers' carbon comes in several colors and works in the same way as ordinary carbon paper.

Pricking and pouncing is one of the oldest methods and is suitable for repeat motifs as only one tracing needs to be made.

Tracing and basting is best for bold designs. A version of this method is used in machine quilting when the outline of the design is stitched directly through the tracing paper.

Preparation of fabric

If the finished embroidery is to be washed, make sure that the fabric is pre-shrunk or wash it before embarking on the project.

Leave at least 2 inches of extra fabric around the design to allow room for adjustments, framing, or mounting.

Positioning the design

The tracing of the design can often be positioned by eye, but for more precise placing, find the center of the tracing by folding it into quarters and mark this point; do the same with the fabric and align both marks.

Direct tracing

Outline the original drawing or tracing in black felt-tip pen. For fine or transparent fabrics, tape the tracing to your work surface, then tape the fabric in position on top. Trace the design with your chosen marker.

Dressmakers' carbon

Tape the fabric to the work surface. Tape the traced design in position on top with dressmakers' carbon paper, colored side down, between the fabric and the tracing. Using a ballpoint pen, draw over the marked lines, pressing firmly.

Pricking and pouncing

Trace the design and turn it over to the reverse side. Place it on a soft surface, such as a piece of felt or a towel. Use a medium-sized needle to prick holes close together along the marked lines. Position the tracing right side up on the fabric and tape it in place.

Make a pouncing pad by rolling up a small rectangle of felt, holding it together by tying a length of thread around it. Dip the end of this into a powder made from crushed dressmakers' chalk and charcoal. Rub the powder through the holes in the tracing paper with a circular movement. Remove the tracing and go over the dotted line lightly with your chosen marker.

Tracing and basting

Trace the design and pin the tracing in position on the fabric. Begin the basting with a knot and a backstitch, and work small running stitches along the lines through both the paper and the fabric. Fasten off securely.

Gently tear away the tracing paper to leave the basted line, which may either be covered with the embroidery or removed as the work progresses.

Frames

For the majority of embroidery techniques, the best results are achieved if the work is mounted in a frame. It will remain clean and uncrumpled, and the tension of the stitches will be even. Whichever type of frame is used, the fabric should first be ironed, backed if necessary, and the design marked ready for stitching. Care should be taken that the fabric is not distorted in any way, but stretched with the warp and weft running at right angles to one another.

Hoops (or ring frames) in wood or metal are available in various sizes and are suitable for small embroidery projects, provided the whole of the design will fit within the bounds of the frame. It is not advisable to relocate the frame to another part of the design, as this may cause damage to previously worked areas.

Stretcher frames consist of four lengths of soft wood with mitered corners, to which the embroidery is fastened with thumbtacks.

Scroll frames come in various types. The most satisfactory are those made of two rollers, each with a tape attached to which the canvas or embroidery background fabric is stitched. The rollers are held apart with side battens which have split pins or pegs to adjust the size.

Ring (or hoop) frames

The inner ring may be bound diagonally with cotton tape to

protect fine or delicate fabrics. This also provides a better grip for free-style machine embroidery.

Adjust the screw of the outer ring so that it fits loosely over the inner ring. Place the fabric

over the inner ring. Press the outer ring down over the fabric and the inner ring, making sure the fabric is straight and taut and the area to be worked is in the center of the ring. Tighten the screw.

Stretcher frames

Mark the center of each side of the frame and make corresponding marks on the fabric. Then, starting at the top edge, align the center marks and secure with a thumbtack. Continue pinning at ½-inch intervals, working toward the

sides. Turn the frame and fasten the bottom edge in a similar way, stretching the fabric taut.

To complete the other two sides, pin the center points and continue toward the ends,

pinning first one side and then the other to equalize the tension of the fabric.

Tapestry (or scroll) frames

Mark the center point of the fabric and fold a ½-inch hem to the wrong side along the top and bottom edges, and a 1-inch hem along the sides. Cut two lengths of string at least 18 inches longer than the side battens. Place these

inside the side hems and machine stitch near the edge to form a casing over each string.

With wrong sides together, align the center points on the top and bottom edges with the center markings on the roller tape. Pin the fabric along the tape and overcast them together with strong, doubled

thread, starting in the center and working toward the edges.

Insert the side battens and secure them with the split pins or pegs so that the fabric is taut. Tie the ends of the strings to the rollers. Lace the sides of the fabric to the side battens using string threaded in a large-eyed needle. Pull the string to tighten the fabric, and tie the ends around the batten ends.

TECHNIQUES

In the past it was usual to work a piece of embroidery using only one technique throughout. However, embroidery has evolved through the 20th century to become very much a means of artistic expression for professional textile artists. Today there are no restrictions on the embroiderer. Several methods can be combined in one piece, and hand-painted and dyed fabrics, handmade paper or found objects can be incorporated with traditional hand- or machine-stitched techniques. This freedom is well within the scope of the amateur and beginner, who need only to master the very basics before being able to design their own work.

SURFACE EMBROIDERY

LINE STITCHES • COUCHING

CHAIN STITCHES

BAND AND BORDER STITCHES

CRETAN AND FEATHER STITCH

SATIN STITCHES

LONG AND SHORT STITCH

RAISED STITCHES • ROUND MOTIFS

ISOLATED STITCHES

CREWEL WORK • INSERTION STITCHES

LAIDWORK

A repertoire of surface stitches is the main element of almost every type of embroidery. Knowing a collection of basic stitches plus a few more unusual ones will enable you to create different effects and work many techniques.

Surface embroidery is sometimes known as free-style embroidery because the stitches are worked independently of the weave of the background fabric, and unlike counted thread embroidery, can be made in any direction and in an infinite variety of yarns.

Stitches can be grouped in a number of ways, to make lines, form circles or create wide bands of pattern. Some are used as small isolated elements sprinkled across the surface, while others may fill a space more solidly.

However, even though a stitch falls into a certain category when used conventionally, it can usually be adapted or modified to produce a different effect. When the working of a stitch has been mastered, it is a good idea to experiment by altering the scale and direction, by working haphazardly or using varying thicknesses and different types of yarn. Some stitches can be over-lapped, while others can be worked in twists, spirals, and circular motifs. This type of experimentation will produce ideas for subjects or elements in a design, and you will find inspiration from the shapes, patterns, and textures which you create with fabric and thread.

Fabrics

Although the traditional fabric used for surface embroidery is either linen or cotton, today's embroiderers are happy to use any background fabric which suits their purpose. For practical articles such as table linens, consideration naturally needs to be given to its uses. But embroidered pictures, panels, and wallhangings present few barriers, and the background may be chosen mainly for its color and texture. For this type of work, the background fabric can be supported on a backing fabric and the embroidery stitched through both layers. For the best results, it is preferable to mount the work in a frame.

Threads

Threads for surface embroidery may include the full range of embroidery threads (page 8) and others such as knitting yarn, crochet cotton, and even string, tape, and ribbon (page 118). In general terms the weight and thickness of the thread should be matched to that of the fabric, but it is often possible to disregard this rule for decorative effect. A variety of yarns can be used for unusual and creative work, provided you can pull the thread through the fabric without distortion.

Needles

Select embroidery needles suitable to the thickness of the yarn, or chenille needles, which have a larger hole for thicker threads.

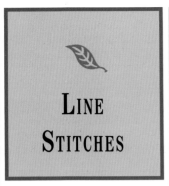

LINE STITCHES

Some of the most useful stitches are those which make thin lines naturally – such as running, stem, chain, and couching. They can be used for defining or outlining shapes as well as for depicting stems of flowers, blades of grass, or branches of trees; worked in flowing lines they will give movement to a design. Rows of line stitches can also be worked close together to fill an area more solidly.

Running stitch, the simplest of all, makes a broken line. This stitch is often seen in hand quilting, but is also useful as a basis for ornamentation combined with whipping and interlacing.

Backstitch forms a continuous thin line similar to machine stitching, while *stem stitch* produces rope-like lines which can vary in thickness depending on the angle at which the needle is inserted.

Running stitch

Working from right to left, bring the needle in and out of the fabric at regular intervals, making evenly spaced stitches. Running stitch can be varied by working stitches of different lengths and with irregular spaces. Solid rows of stitching can be built up to give a flat texture.

Whipped running stitch

Work a row of evenly spaced running stitches. Starting with a new thread in a tapestry needle, bring the needle up alongside the first stitch and take it through the next stitch, but not through the fabric. Repeat. Variations can be made by using a contrasting thread for whipping or by altering the length and spacing of the running stitches. Multiple rows of running stitch can also be whipped.

Interlaced running stitch

Work a row of evenly spaced running stitches. Using a tapestry needle and another thread, take the needle alternately up and down through the stitches, but not through the fabric. A third thread can be interlaced similarly from the reverse direction. Multiple rows of running stitches can also be interlaced.

Backstitch

Bring the needle up at A, a short distance from the starting point (B), then take it down at the starting point and bring it out ahead of A at C. This makes a smooth, continuous row of stitching suitable for outlines and for blackwork and Italian quilting.

Pekinese stitch

Work a line of backstitch. Using a tapestry needle, bring the needle out at A and take it up through the next but one backstitch (but not through the fabric) and back down through the previous backstitch to form a circular loop. The tension may be loose or tight, but should be kept even.

Stem stitch

Working from left to right, bring the needle up at A, take it down at B along the stitching line, and bring it up at C halfway between A and B. For the second stitch, insert the needle at D. While working, keep the thread either above or below the stitching line.

The thickness of stem stitch can be varied by taking the stitch diagonally across the stitching line.

Split stitch

This is worked in a similar way to stem stitch, but the needle is brought up halfway through the previous stitch, splitting the thread.

Split stitch produces a thin line which is useful for filling spaces, or as a preparatory outline stitch for satin or long and short stitch.

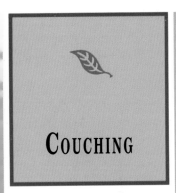

COUCHING

Couched threads are those which are laid on the surface and secured by means of a series of small stitches made over them, usually worked at regular intervals.

Couching, used for metal thread work and for attaching yarns which are too thick or textured to go through the background, is a versatile method; the type of threads and couching stitches can be varied to produce many different effects. It is essential to work couching on fabric which is tautly framed.

Couching

Bring the thread to be couched out at the start of the stitching line, remove the needle, and use your non-stitching hand to hold the thread taut on the fabric. Bring the couching thread through a little way along the stitching line at A and take a small vertical stitch over the laid thread to B. Repeat to the end of the stitching line and fasten off. Rethread the couched thread, take it through to the back of the work, and fasten off. If the couched thread is very thick, pull it through with pliers and secure with a few stitches using fine thread.

Pendant couching

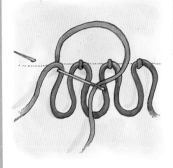

Pendant couching is worked in a similar way to couching except that the couching stitches are worked fairly close together and the laid thread is left loose to form a loop.

Trailing

In this form of couching, the laid thread is completely covered by couching stitches worked close together and taking up as little of the background fabric as possible so that a raised cord is produced.

CHAIN STITCHES

Chain stitch and its variations are all based on bringing the working thread through the loop to produce a slightly raised line. Tension is important in order to retain the chain effect, but simple *chain stitch* can be worked evenly or with loops of different sizes. *Whipped chain* gives a raised rope-like line, while *open chain,* as its name implies, recreates a wide open line.

Rosette chain has a pretty textured braid effect and can also be stitched in circular formation to produce flower shapes (page 29).

Twisted chain is worked in a similar way to chain stitch, except that the needle is inserted to the side of the loop. If twisted chain is embroidered very small with a longer stitch between the loops, it produces *coral stitch.*

Double knot stitch is similar in effect to coral stitch but with heavier knots.

Chain stitch

Work this stitch toward you from top to bottom. Bring the needle up at A and insert it again into the same hole, leaving a loop. Bring the needle up through the loop on the stitching line at B. Repeat. To finish, take a vertical stitch to secure the loop.

Whipped chain stitch

Work a row of chain stitch. Then, using a coordinating or contrasting thread in a tapestry needle, bring the needle up alongside the first stitch and take it under the loop, but not through the fabric. Repeat through the next stitch.

Open chain stitch

This is worked in a similar way to chain stitch, but in a wider form. Bring the needle up at A, insert it at B, leaving a loop, and bring it out at C, leaving the thread loose. Take the needle down at D inside the loop and bring it out again at E. Repeat. To finish, take two vertical stitches to secure the final loop.

Twisted chain stitch

This is worked in a similar way to chain stitch except that the needle is inserted outside the loop to the left of A and brought through the loop at B, forming the twist.

Repeat the process as above.

Coral stitch

This is worked in a similar way to twisted chain stitch except that the needle is taken horizontally across the stitching line, from A, emerging through the loop at B to form a small knot. Repeat a short distance away from the first knot.

Rosette chain

Work this stitch from right to left. Begin with a single twisted chain stitch. Slide the needle up through the first part of the stitch, but not through the fabric. Repeat.

Double knot stitch

Bring the needle up at A and take up a small amount of fabric across the stitching line from B to C. Slip the needle under the vertical stitch and pull the thread tight.

Work a chain stitch through the vertical stitch, but not through the fabric.

BAND & BORDER STITCHES

When worked conventionally, this group of stitches produces wide borders or bands of texture. All the stitches, however, can be adapted and worked freely to produce some of the most interesting effects in the embroiderer's repertoire.

Buttonhole, also known as blanket stitch, is extremely versatile – it can be used for edgings as in cutwork (page 111) and appliqué (page 88), or as a decorative stitch in its own right, when it can be worked evenly or at random to produce many different effects. *Buttonhole wheels* are made by stitching in a circle (page 29).

Herringbone stitch can be embroidered in a very regular fashion with even spaces which may be apart or very close together. It can also serve as a basis for embellishment by interlacing or threading as in *threaded herringbone*.

Buttonhole stitch

Bring the needle out at A, insert it at B above the stitching line, and bring it out again at C through the loop. Repeat, starting again at B. To finish, secure with a small stitch to hold the loop.

Up-and-down buttonhole

Work a single buttonhole stitch. Insert the needle at A and bring it out at B alongside the first stitch and through the loop. Repeat and finish as for buttonhole stitch.

Herringbone stitch

Working from left to right, bring the needle out at A on the lower stitching line and take a diagonal stitch to B. Bring the needle out at C a short distance left of B and take a diagonal stitch in the other direction to D. Bring the needle out at E to repeat.

Close herringbone stitch

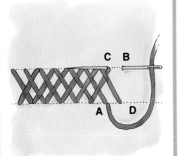

This is worked in a similar way to herringbone stitch but close together, with the stitches touching one another.

Threaded herringbone stitch

Over a foundation line of herringbone stitch, work a contrasting thread (not through the fabric), lacing it up and down across the intersections.

▲ **Pauline Brown**
This sample shows the use of herringbone, worked closely for the background area and freely for the wheat.

CRETAN AND FEATHER STITCH

Open Cretan stitch

Closed Cretan stitch

Evenly worked in a similar way to herringbone stitch, *open Cretan stitch* forms a zigzag line, but when stitched freely in overlapping formation, interesting textures can be built up. It is often used for depicting grasses, and worked vertically it is useful for shadows or water effects.

Closed Cretan is stitched in a similar way, but more fabric is picked up for each stitch, which produces a central plait. Worked as a filling stitch, it is especially good for leaves and other motifs requiring a ridge down the center.

The whole range of *feather stitches*, particularly *closed feather*, is suitable for decorative borders. *Single* and *double feather* can be stitched haphazardly to create vegetation such as trees and bushes.

Bring the needle up at A on the lower stitching line. Insert it at B above and slightly to the right and bring it out directly below at C, keeping the thread to the right. Then insert the needle at D and bring it up at E, still keeping the thread on the right.

This is worked in a similar way to open Cretan, but with the stitches worked closer together to cover the fabric.

▼ Daphne J. Ashby
Sheep
This piece demonstrates the free use of Cretan stitch. Different effects can be achieved by taking up more or less amounts of fabric and by varying the distances between each stitch. You can also overlap rows of stitches to build up a textured surface.

Feather stitch

Bring the needle up at A, insert it at B, and keeping the thread toward you, bring it up at C through the loop. Repeat the stitch below and to the left, at D and E, then work another to the right. Repeat.

Double feather stitch

This is stitched in a similar way to single, but two stitches are worked to the right and left alternately. This stitch can be varied by altering the distances between stitches and the angle at which they are worked.

Closed feather stitch

The formation of this variation is similar to single feather stitch. Bring the needle up at A, insert it at B, and bring it up at C through the loop. Insert the needle just below A, bring it up at D, insert it just below C, and bring it out at E.

▲ **Pauline Brown**
Feather stitch is ideal for depicting the delicate tracery of this willow.

SATIN STITCHES

Satin stitch is especially beautiful when it is worked in pure silk floss or other threads which reflect the light to give the characteristic smooth, shiny look.

Although at first sight it seems quite easy, it is actually one of the most difficult stitches to work well: the individual stitches need to be embroidered exactly parallel to one another with the threads lying smoothly. In order to preserve a well-defined shape, satin stitch should be embroidered at an angle wherever possible. An outline of split stitch (page 16) with the satin stitch worked on top will help to keep the edge smooth.

The length of stitches should be limited as they may become unwieldy and liable to snag; large areas should be broken up.

Padded satin gives a raised effect suitable for a small area, such as the center of a flower, with a second layer of satin stitch worked over the first row.

Satin or padded satin stitch are commonly used for monograms on napkins, handkerchiefs, or other fine linens.

Satin stitch

Bring the needle up at A on one edge of the shape to be covered, and insert it at B, diagonally across on the opposite edge. Bring the needle up at C, immediately next to A, and insert it at D.

Padded satin stitch

Fill the area with satin stitch and then work a second layer on top at right angles to the first. For a more raised effect, a third layer can be stitched.

Voiding

This is a characteristic of Chinese embroidery, in which areas of satin stitch, often worked on a dark background, are stitched with a narrow but clearly defined space between.

Encroaching satin stitch

This is a useful method for filling an area, with subsequent rows worked slightly into the previous ones, producing an interlocked woven effect.

◄ **Nancy Martin**
This treatment of solidly worked satin stitch is unusual.

LONG AND SHORT STITCH

Long and short stitch is most often used for shading motifs such as petals and leaves and can create very realistic effects. Practice is required to perfect a smooth gradation both of stitching and color.

This stitch is worked in a similar way to satin, but the first row has stitches of unequal length, with subsequent rows interlocking. A rectangular area is relatively simple to cover in this way, but with shapes which diminish in size, such as petals, it is trickier, as the number and size of the stitches will gradually diminish.

Long and short stitch

1 For a rectangular shape, begin with a row of long and short vertical stitches worked alternately.

2 The second and subsequent rows are made with stitches of equal length fitting into the spaces.

Shaping and shading

1 Define the outside edge of a shape such as a petal with the first row of long and short stitch in a dark color. Begin in the center at A and work to the right before returning to the center and working to the left. The stitches should converge toward the center of the flower.

2 For subsequent rows in gradually changing shades, work equal-length stitches between. It is necessary to eliminate some stitches as the shape dictates.

RAISED STITCHES

The textural effect of raised embroidery stitches can quite literally bring another dimension to creative work.

Raised chain and *stem bands* are both worked on a "ladder" of straight stitches which may be of even or uneven width and spaced uniformly or randomly. The chain and stem stitches are then worked on the ladder foundation, either in single or multiple rows. Thick or textured threads can be used if desired as they only have to be inserted through the background fabric at the start and the finish.

Buttonhole loops look best when massed together, while *raised herringbone* is usually worked as an individual motif or grouped in a flower or leaf form. *Woven picots* were originally made as a minute triangular edging stitch, but nowadays are often used to depict leaves.

Raised chain band

1 Make a series of evenly spaced horizontal straight stitches. Using a contrasting thread in a tapestry needle, bring the needle up at A just above the center of the first stitch.

Bring the needle over and up under the first stitch to the left (not through the fabric).

2 Then bring the needle down under the first stitch to the right of the working thread and pull through the loop. Repeat, keeping the tension even.

Raised stem band

Work a narrow ladder of stitches as for raised chain band. Bring the needle out at A above the first horizontal stitch.

Then bring the needle over and up under the first stitch to the right (as for conventional stem stitch, but not through the fabric). Repeat. For best effect, work several rows.

Buttonhole loops

Make a bar with two or three loose straight stitches one on top of the other.

Then work a series of buttonhole stitches (page 20) to cover the foundation bar (but not through the fabric). Depending on the length and looseness of the bar, different effects can be created.

Raised herringbone stitch

Make a small vertical straight stitch. Bring the needle up at A below and to the left of this, take it through the straight stitch (but not through the fabric) and insert it at B to the right on a level with A. Bring the needle out at C, just above A, and repeat the stitch three or four times to produce a leaf shape.

Woven picots

1 Insert a pin to take up as much fabric as the finished size of the picot. Bring the needle out at A to the left of the pin and take the thread around the top of the pin and insert the needle at B. Bring the needle out again at C, and take the thread around the top of the pin as before. Begin weaving on this foundation of three threads, taking the needle under, over and under on the first run. Then weave from left to right over, under, and over.

2 Continue until the base of the picot is reached. Maintain a loose tension so that the triangular form of the picot is preserved.

ROUND MOTIFS

Circular stitches are ideal for motifs such as flowers, berries, or wheels. Although many stitches, such as chain or satin stitch, can of course be worked to form a round shape, there are a number which naturally produce circular motifs. *Woven wheels* and *woven spider's webs* are both embroidered on a foundation of straight stitches radiating from a central point, with woven wheels having a smooth texture and spider's webs being more knobbly.

Raised cup is more unusual. This is worked on a base of backstitch in a type of twisted buttonhole stitch, producing a small raised circular outline.

Rosette chain (page 19) can be stitched in a ring to create a pretty flower shape, and *buttonhole stitch* (page 20), well-known for its versatility, can be embroidered with the loop either at the center of the circle or on the outer edge.

Woven wheels

Work a circle of seven straight stitches radiating from a central point. Using a tapestry needle and a long thread, bring the needle up at A near the center of the circle. Take the needle alternately under and over the straight stitches until the circle is filled.

Woven spider's webs

Make a foundation circle of any number of straight stitches as for woven wheels. Bring the needle up at A near the center of the circle. Take the needle under two radiating stitches (but not through the fabric), back over the second thread, and then under both it and the next one. Proceed with this backstitch movement (page 16) around the circle, gradually loosening the tension until the radiating stitches are covered.

Variations on woven wheels and spider's webs
The number and length of the base threads can be altered, and they can be left partly uncovered if desired. Colors and textures can also be varied to provide added interest.

Raised cup stitch

Work a foundation of three backstitches (page 16) in triangular formation. Bring the needle up at A just outside the triangle. Work a series of twisted buttonhole stitches from right to left on the backstitch foundation (but not through the fabric) until a tiny raised circle is achieved.

Rosette chain wheel

Work a series of rosette chain stitches (page 19) to form a circular motif.

Buttonhole wheels

Working with the loop on the outside, stitch a series of buttonhole stitches (page 20) to form a circle. Half and quarter circles can also be created. For a spiky effect, work with the loop at the center of the circle. The length of the stitches can also be varied.

▼ **Pauline Brown**
Woven and rosette chain wheels form the flower heads, and the leaves are worked in buttonhole stitch.

ISOLATED STITCHES

There are a number of detached stitches which can be used individually as tiny motifs or scattered across an area to make patterns or alter the tone of the background. If massed together, these stitches will create texture, or when grouped can form decorative motifs.

French and *bullion knots* are often used for the centers of flowers, and they can both be worked with "tails," which can simulate stamens or tiny trees. Bullion knots can be varied by stitching them on a loose thread, giving an effect similar to buttonhole loops (page 27).

Detached chain stitch, also known as daisy stitch or lazy daisy, is usually embroidered in a flower shape, while *wheatear* and *fern stitch* are both useful additions for floral subjects.

Fly stitch seems at first sight to be very ordinary, but in fact is extremely versatile, as the length of the "tail" and the appearance can be varied to produce different shapes.

French knots

Bring the needle out at A, hold the thread taut between the index finger and thumb of your non-stitching hand and twist the needle around the thread twice. Insert the needle halfway at B, pull the twist down the needle so that it lies on the fabric, then push the needle through to the back of the work.

Bullion knots

Bring the needle out at A. Insert it the required length of the stitch at B, bringing it halfway out again at A. Twist the thread around the needle about six times, then hold the twist with your thumb, and pull the needle and thread through both the fabric and the twist. Pull the needle and thread back toward B and insert the needle at B.

Detached chain stitch

Bring the needle up at A and insert it again into the same hole, leaving a loop. Bring it up through the loop on the stitching line at B. To finish, take a vertical stitch to secure the loop. This last stitch can be tiny or quite long.

Variations

Both French knots and bullion knots can be worked with tails. In each case, after forming the knot, insert the needle a short distance away. Bullion loops can be made by inserting the needle a tiny distance away from the starting point and winding the thread around the needle many times.

Wheatear stitch

Make two small straight stitches in the form of a V. Bring the needle out at A a short distance below the V, pass it through the straight stitches (but not through the fabric), and insert it again at A. This can also be used as a continuous decorative line stitch.

Fern stitch

Make three small straight stitches all radiating from the central hole. This can also be used as a continuous line stitch.

Fly stitch

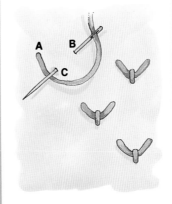

This is worked in a similar way to detached chain, except that the needle is brought up at A, inserted a small distance away at B, and brought up again through the loop at C. The fastening stitch can be long or short.

Variations

Detached chain can be doubled in size by working another around the first, while wheatear can be thickened with an extra loop stitched through the straight stitches. Fly stitch and detached chain can both be worked with long or short tails.

▲ **Pauline Brown**
Fly stitch in raffia and stranded floss forms a stylized tree.

INSERTION STITCHES

Although insertion stitches are seldom seen now in their traditional role – as a decorative means of joining sections of garments together – they are an interesting group of stitches and can be used inventively on wallhangings and embroidered panels to hold areas of the design or different fabrics together.

The folded-back hems of the fabrics must first be joined onto a firm backing such as strong paper, and the insertion stitches are then worked on the surface across the gap. Yarns such as coton à broder, pearl cotton, or crochet cotton are the most suitable as the threads will not separate.

Faggoting, or twisted insertion, is the most familiar stitch, producing a zigzag effect, as does *knotted insertion*. An easy type of insertion can be made with groups of *buttonhole stitch* (page 20) worked alternately on the upper and lower edges of the fabric.

Preparation for insertion stitches

The edges of two pieces of fabric between which the insertion stitch is to be worked must first be folded over and hemmed in place. To preserve good tension and evenness of stitch, baste them to a base of firm paper, leaving a space of from ¼ inch to 1 inch according to the width of the required insertion stitch.

Faggoting

Working from left to right, bring the needle up at A, take it across the space and up again at B. From the right. pass the needle under and over the thread and bring it up again at C. Repeat.

Buttonhole insertion stitch

Bring the needle out at A and work three or four buttonhole stitches over the folded edge of the fabric. Take the thread diagonally across the space to the opposite folded edge and work another set of buttonhole stitches. Repeat. The effect of this stitch can be varied by altering the height of the buttonhole stitches or leaving more or less space between them.

Knotted insertion stitch

The knotted stitch is worked alternately from edge to edge. Bring the needle up from the back of the fabric at A and insert it further along to the right at B, making a diagonal stitch and keeping the thread to the right; then make a buttonhole stitch loop to secure the diagonal thread. Take the thread diagonally across to the other edge and repeat the knotted stitch on the other edge.

▶ **Pauline Brown**
An insertion stitch sampler has been applied to backgrounds of different colors.

CREWEL WORK

Crewel work, traditionally worked in fine "crewel" yarn on linen, is one of the earliest forms of English surface embroidery. It was very popular in 17th-century England – it is sometimes known as Jacobean embroidery – and was also used by William Morris and his followers in the late 19th century.

▲ **Joanne Dixey**
This crewel work is stitched in traditional Jacobean style.

Fabrics
Natural linen or linen crash are the traditional fabrics, but other materials with weaves suitable to take fine wool yarns can also be used. The fabric should be framed to accommodate the intricate filling stitches.

Threads
Fine tapestry or crewel yarn are most often used, but other yarns may be chosen for a contemporary approach.

Needles
Crewel (or embroidery) needles are the most satisfactory.

Designs
Crewel work is characterized by its linear form combined with areas such as leaves and flowers filled with decorative stitches. Transfer the design by direct tracing (page 10), transfer pen, or dressmakers' carbon paper.

Stitches
Crewel work incorporates many of the most familiar embroidery stitches, but there are several which are particular to this technique, including *trellis* and *honeycomb filling*, both of which make decorative fillings. *Tête-de-boeuf* is an isolated motif stitch which can be scattered in a pattern, while *battlement couching* produces a three-dimensional effect.

Trellis stitch

1 Make a row of parallel horizontal straight stitches by bringing the needle up at A, inserting it at B, bringing it up again at C, and inserting it at D. Repeat and then work a similar row on top at right angles to the first.

2 Using a similar or contrasting thread, make small diagonal straight stitches over each inter-section. This stitch can be further elaborated with stitches such as cross, detached chain, French knots, etc., in some or all the spaces.

Other stitches for crewel work
Buttonhole stitch (page 20)   Fly stitch (page 31)
Chain stitch (page 17)   French knots (page 30)
Twisted chain (page 19)   Bullion knots (page 30)
Couching (page 17)   Laidwork (page 36)
Satin stitch (page 24)
Long and short stitch
  (page 25)

Honeycomb filling stitch

1 Work a series of parallel horizontal straight stitches as for trellis stitch. Stitch a second row of diagonal stitches on top of the first.

2 For the third layer, bring the needle out at A, and then take it across to B, weaving under and over the first two layers of stitches to achieve the honeycomb effect.

Tête-de-boeuf stitch

Make a single detached chain stitch (page 30) between two straight stitches set at a right angle to one another. This stitch is normally worked in a half-drop formation to form a decorative filling.

Battlement couching

1 To achieve the most effective result, the layers of stitches should be worked in threads which are graded in tone. Make a grid of vertical straight stitches from A to F with horizontal ones crossing them from G to L.

2 Lay another grid of stitches in a different color, on the right of the vertical stitches and above the horizontal.

3 Repeat and secure the top grid with small diagonal stitches across the intersections.

LAIDWORK

Notably found in oriental silk embroidery and English crewel work, laidwork consists of a series of couched lines worked side by side to fill a space. Originally developed as an economical method of using precious silk or metal, the laid base threads are secured decoratively in a selection of different patterns.

The laidwork base differs from satin stitch in that the underneath stitches do not cover the back of the fabric, but are taken along the edge of the shape to be stitched. *Romanian* and *Bokhara couching* are similarly worked, by laying threads and securing them in one process. For Romanian couching, a stitch is taken across the space and held down with long diagonal stitches on the return journey. As the work progresses, the tying stitches are worked to form a textured surface, so that the laid stitches are indistinguishable from those holding them. Bokhara couching is embroidered in a similar way, but the tying stitches are shorter and usually form an overall diagonal pattern.

Fabrics
If laidwork stitches are incorporated in a crewel work design (page 34), the natural choice would be linen or linen crash. For silk embroidery, a more delicate fabric, such as silk or satin mounted on a cotton backing, is more appropriate.

Threads
Use crewel yarn for crewel designs, and stranded floss or floss silk for oriental-type embroidery.

Needles
Use crewel or embroidery needles of appropriate size.

Laid base

Make a series of straight vertical stitches parallel to one another from A to B and C to D. Care should be taken that the top and bottom edges are even and that the background fabric is covered.

Straight stitch laidwork

On a laid base, work a series of small straight stitches to hold individual or pairs of laid threads in place to create a surface pattern. These can be stitched in straight lines, brick formation, scallops, or diamonds.

Laidwork trellis

1 Over a laid base, work a grid of diagonal stitches as for trellis stitch (page 34).

2 Secure these with a small stitch worked at each intersection.

Romanian couching

This is normally used as a filling stitch, but occasionally it is also used as a border. Embroider a straight stitch across the area to be filled, bring the needle up at A and insert it at B, making a long, obliquely slanting stitch to give a woven appearance.

Bokhara couching

Work a straight stitch as for Romanian couching. For the first tying stitch, bring the needle out at A, make a small diagonal stitch to B, continue with similar diagonal stitches at regular intervals.

▲ **Pamela Rooke**
Laidwork is used here to create the solidity of the robes.

NEEDLEPOINT

BASIC TECHNIQUE

CROSSED STITCHES

DIAGONAL STITCHES

EYELETS

SQUARE STITCHES

LEAVES AND FLOWERS

TEXTURED STITCHES

BARGELLO EMBROIDERY

FOUR-WAY BARGELLO

Of all embroidery techniques, needlepoint is perhaps the most popular. Also known as canvaswork, or tapestry – the latter because it was developed as a stitched imitation of woven tapestry – it has been practiced since the 16th century. It achieved widespread use in the 19th century when Berlin woolwork, as it was then known, was stitched for all types of articles from slippers and smoking caps to upholstery on chairs and footstools. This work was done solely in tent (or half-cross) stitch, but today's embroiderers prefer to extend the range of stitches and threads to produce a wide variety of raised, patterned, and textural effects.

Canvas
Single or double canvas (page 9) can be used depending on the type of stitch, the design, and the practical use (if any) to which the finished piece will be put.

Threads
Tapestry, Persian, and crewel yarn are most often chosen for needlepoint, but different textures and fibers, such as stranded floss and pearl cotton or knitting and crochet yarns can add interest to a design. Ribbons and tapes can also be used experimentally. Threads should be chosen to fit the gauge of the canvas and also the type of stitch – vertical stitches do not cover the canvas as well as those which are worked diagonally.

Needles
Tapestry needles come in sizes from 13 to 24. Select a size which slides easily between the canvas mesh.

Frames
It is essential to frame needlepoint embroidery, as distortion is likely to occur if the work is stitched in the hand, particularly with diagonal stitches. Rectangular handheld or floorstanding frames are available, or you can use a wooden stretcher with the canvas pinned in place. Round embroidery hoops are not suitable.

Designs
Very many types of design are suitable for translating into needlepoint. The canvas mesh makes it an ideal medium for geometric designs which can be worked out on a line chart (page 39). Pictorial and abstract subjects with areas of the design filled with different stitches are also popular. Although commercially produced kits often have the entire design painted onto the canvas, for more spontaneous and creative work you only need to mark the outlines so that areas can be filled with a variety of stitches.

PREPARATION

Preparing the canvas

Cut the canvas along the threads and make sure that the corners are square. If a stretcher frame is being used, bind all four edges with masking tape; when working on a slate frame, bind the side edges only.

For geometric designs, mark the center of the canvas with vertical and horizontal lines using a waterproof marking pen.

Transferring the design

Outline the main lines of the design with a black felt-tip pen and tape it to your work surface. Position and tape the canvas centrally on top of the design and then trace the design using a waterproof marker. Details can be added as the needlepoint proceeds. For more elaborate designs, the canvas can be painted, using a little paint and a fairly dry brush. Use a waterproof paint such as fabric paint or acrylic.

Following a line chart

On this type of chart, the lines represent the threads of the canvas, with the stitches drawn between or diagonally across the grid. The stitches are then worked vertically, horizontally or diagonally to correspond to the diagram.

When stitching, always count the number of canvas threads or intersections over which the stitch is worked. Bring the needle up at A and insert it at B, and so on.

▶ **Jenifer Murray**
Plus ça change, plus c'est la même chose
This geometric needlepoint design includes a wide variety of stitches.

BASIC TECHNIQUE

Working needlepoint in a frame makes it much faster as well as preventing distortion. One hand is used to push the needle into the canvas from above with a stabbing movement, while the other, below the canvas, pulls it through.

Only a short length of yarn should be used as the canvas tends to wear out the fibers as stitching proceeds. If possible, the needle should come up through an empty hole and go down in one which is partially filled by a previous stitch. The loose ends at the beginning and end of the stitching are woven into the previously worked area.

Tent stitch, also called petit point and half-cross stitch, is the best known and most popular stitch. It can be used for detailed work, for flat areas of a design, or as a *compensating stitch,* to fill in small areas between other stitches. It is also used over *tramming* to give a hard-wearing, ridged appearance. Other basic needlepoint stitches include *cross-stitch, Gobelin, Parisian,* and *Hungarian* stitches. The last three are worked vertically with the yarn lying between the upright threads of the canvas, making it essential to use a yarn which is thick enough to cover the canvas.

Tent stitch

This is the smallest needle-point stitch, worked over one intersection of canvas. Each stitch is made from top right to bottom left. This produces a long thread at the back between stitches which makes the work hard-wearing. For the second row, starting at the right, each stitch is worked from bottom left to top right.

Diagonal tent stitch

This is worked diagonally from top left down to bottom right. The first stitch is made over one intersection, as for tent stitch. Subsequent similar stitches are made diagonally below. For the second row, begin at the bottom, to the left of the first row and work upward, filling in the spaces.

◀ **Susan Smith**
Oakgates
Tent stitch and Gobelin stitch successfully depict the details on the house and in the sky.

Tramming

This is a long horizontal stitch laid along the double threads of a canvas as a base over which the tent, Gobelin, or other stitches are worked.

Gobelin stitch

This straight stitch, named for the tapestries of that name, can be worked in a variety of ways, either upright or slightly slanting and stitched over a differing number of horizontal, as well as vertical, threads.

Parisian stitch

This consists of alternating long and short vertical stitches, usually worked over four and two threads respectively. In the second row, the long stitches are worked directly below the short stitches of the previous row, and vice versa.

Hungarian stitch

This forms a half-drop pattern suitable for backgrounds. It consists of groups of three vertical stitches, worked over two, four, and again two threads. Two vertical threads are left between each group, into which subsequent rows are interlocked.

Compensating stitches
For pictorial and abstract designs containing irregular or curved shapes, it may not be possible to fill the entire area with a given stitch. Compensating stitches are those which are worked to fill in the gaps around the edges. It is essential to retain the form of the stitch as much as possible, working half or a part of it. Tent stitch is often the best solution for small spaces.

CROSSED STITCHES

Basic cross stitch is well known, but is only one of a number of stitches where threads cross. In each case the top threads should all lie in the same direction, unless there is some esthetic reason to contradict this rule.

Variations can be made in size and shape – *long-legged, upright cross, herringbone,* and *tied Gobelin* are elongated or irregular versions – while others, such as *plaited Gobelin* encroach on the previous row to form the cross.

Areas of crossed stitches produce different textures, from the smoothness of single cross stitch to the raised braid effects of long-legged cross and herringbone stitch. Some, such as upright cross, can combine with other stitches to fill in gaps or can be worked in two colors.

Cross stitch

Two diagonal straight stitches are worked over two intersections of canvas at right angles to one another. Complete each cross before starting the next. If you are working a long row of cross stitch, you may prefer to make the first half of the stitches for one row, and then complete them by working back along the row in the opposite direction. Larger versions are unlikely to cover the canvas satisfactorily, so they may need to be interspersed with other stitches.

Upright cross stitch

Also known as straight cross stitch, this makes a good texture for backgrounds. It consists of a vertical and a horizontal stitch worked to form a cross over two threads of canvas. The second row of crosses is worked to interlock between those in the first row.

Plaited Gobelin stitch

Starting at the bottom left-hand side of the stitch, work a row of slanting Gobelin stitches (page 41) over one vertical and four horizontal threads. The second row slants in the opposite direction, starting three threads below, and crossing the first row. The length and slant of this stitch can be varied.

Tied Gobelin stitch

Work a slanting stitch over five horizontal and two vertical threads of canvas. Secure it at its center with a small stitch made obliquely over one horizontal and two vertical threads. Each long stitch is worked with a space of two threads between it and the next, and the second row of stitches is placed directly below, encroaching by two horizontal threads.

Long-legged cross stitch

Starting at the bottom left-hand corner of the stitch, take a diagonal stitch over three horizontal and six vertical threads. Bring the needle out immediately below this point and on a level with the starting point. Take a cross stitch diagonally back over three vertical and three horizontal threads. Repeat.

Herringbone stitch

This is similar to surface embroidery herringbone (page 20). Work a diagonal stitch to the right over four intersections of canvas. Then bring the needle out again two vertical threads to the left before making another diagonal stitch, again over four intersections and crossing the first. The second row is worked directly below and encroaches into the first.

▲ **Elizabeth Ashurst**
House on the Hill
Tent, cross, Gobelin, and velvet stitch feature in this piece.

DIAGONAL STITCHES

In this group of stitches, each individual stitch is worked diagonally, and the stitches *en masse* form diagonal patterns of varying complexity across the canvas.

Diagonal, cashmere, and *Moorish* stitches are suitable for covering areas of background in an unobtrusive manner, while *Milanese, Jacquard,* and *Byzantine* are bolder and can be quite striking, especially if the rows are worked in contrasting threads.

Diagonal stitches are usually shown worked from top left to bottom right, but they can be stitched in the other direction by reversing the instructions.

Diagonal stitch

The smaller version of this stitch is made up of diagonal stitches taken over one and two intersections of canvas alternately. The larger version consists of groups of four diagonal stitches worked over two, three, four, and three intersections, which are then repeated. Subsequent rows interlock.

Moorish stitch

This is an attractive background stitch which can be worked in one or two colors. Rows of large diagonal stitch are interspersed with rows of diagonal tent stitch (page 40).

Cashmere stitch

Depending on the effect required, you can vary the slanted line of this stitch. Repeated groups of diagonal stitches are worked alongside one another over one, two, and again two intersections of canvas. Subsequent rows are interlocked with those previously worked.

Milanese stitch

This consists of triangles made up of groups of diagonal stitches worked over one, two, three, and four intersections. These are repeated along the diagonal, with subsequent rows reversed and interlocked, with the shortest stitch opposite the longest on the previous row.

Byzantine stitch

This stitch gives the effect of a series of steps, usually worked from top left. The length, width, and direction of the steps may be varied. Five diagonal stitches are made alongside one another over four intersections; then four are worked downward to form the zigzag. Continue stitching the groups of four stitches, alternating horizontal and vertical.

Jacquard stitch

This is a stepped stitch similar to Byzantine, usually with the larger stitches worked over four intersections of canvas. These steps are separated by rows of tent stitch (page 40). As with Byzantine stitch, the height, width, and direction of the zigzags can be varied.

▶ **Pauline Brown**
Byzantine and Jacquard stitches are worked in different directions on this sampler.

EYELETS

Eyelets are normally worked in a square over an even number of threads in each directon. The stitches are taken from the outer edge of the square down into the central hole. To keep the center well defined, it is sometimes necessary to enlarge it slightly with a stiletto before beginning. The thread chosen for eyelets should be fairly fine and tightly spun, so that it will not create too much bulk in the center hole.

Square and *rectangular eyelets* can both be worked in the normal way or varied by moving the hole off-center and working over any number of threads.

Diamond eyelets form a half-drop pattern when stitched in rows. They can be outlined with straight stitches to emphasize the diamond effect.

Fan stitch is worked in a similar way to eyelets, except that the stitches fan out from the corner hole. It can be worked in any direction, producing a variety of different patterns.

Circular eyelets can be used as individual motifs, such as flowers, or as an all-over pattern, either in one color or in a range of hues.

Square eyelets

Starting at the top right-hand corner, work radiating stitches in a counterclockwise direction around a square consisting of an even number of threads. Take the needle down into the center hole for each stitch and bring it up at the edge of the square.

Diamond eyelets

These are worked in a similar way to conventional square eyelets. The vertical and horizontal stitches are made over five threads of canvas, with the other stitches between worked diagonally into the center hole. Diamond eyelets can be used individually to represent flowers or can be used as an all-over pattern, sometimes outlined with long diagonal stitches.

Fan stitch

Fan stitch is usually worked over three vertical and three horizontal threads of canvas. It is actually a quarter of a square eyelet, with stitches radiating from a corner hole. The direction and size of the stitch can be varied.

Circular eyelets

These are stitched in a similar way to conventional square eyelets. However, they form an octagonal shape, consisting of 16 radiating stitches. The whole stitch is worked over six horizontal and six vertical threads of canvas – each side of the octagon has three radiating stitches.

Variation on circular eyelets

Circular eyelets can be worked side by side with subsequent rows interlocking to produce an all-over pattern. If the second row is worked immediately below the first, the resultant spaces can be filled with smaller eyelets.

Eyelet variations
Eyelets are so versatile that it is worth experimenting with different sizes and shapes.

▲ **Eyelet ribbon embroidery**
Pauline Brown
Narrow satin and metallic ribbons are worked on canvas using conventional needlepoint stitches with French knots added.

SQUARE STITCHES

A number of needlepoint stitches have a square shape as their main characteristic, which makes them suitable, among other things, for creating architectural features such as stone or brickwork.

Cushion stitch is especially versatile, as it can be worked in either direction and any size. Large-scale versions can be varied further with an additional stitch or series of stitches worked across in the other direction to form *crossed cushion stitch.*

When cushion stitch is outlined with tent stitch, it becomes *Scotch stitch,* which is useful for depicting windows or tiles.

Rice stitch, also known as crossed corners, is worked in two stages over an even number of threads. A contrasting color can be used for the corner stitches.

Smyrna or double cross stitch is also stitched over an even number of threads. It should be kept to a small size to cover the canvas adequately.

Cushion stitch

Groups of diagonal stitches are worked over first one, two, three, and four, then three, two, and one intersections to form a square. Variations can be made in size or direction.

Crossed cushion stitch

There are two versions of this stitch, in each case worked on top of individual cushion stitches or groups of the required size. The first variation consists of a single diagonal stitch worked in the reverse direction from corner to corner over cushion stitch. For a padded effect, half of the cushion stitch can be covered with diagonal stitches worked in the reverse direction.

Scotch stitch

Rows of cushion stitch are separated with a grid of tent stitch. The size of the cushion stitch and the colors used can be varied to produce a more random effect.

Rice stitch

Work a large cross stitch (page 42) over four intersections of canvas. Then work small diagonal stitches over two intersections across each corner. Slight variations in size and color can be made.

Smyrna stitch

This consists of a cross stitch (page 42) worked over two or four intersections of canvas, with an upright cross stitch (page 42) stitched on top. If worked conventionally, the top stitches should all lie in one direction, either horizontal or vertical.

◄ **Anna Christy**
Rhodes Fragment II
Cushion and fan stitch are included in this piece, which has been machine embroidered on a linen background.

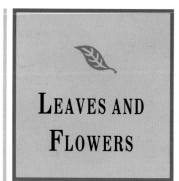

LEAVES AND FLOWERS

Many embroiderers enjoy creating needlepoint pictures of gardens and floral subjects. In addition to circular and diamond eyelets (page 46), a number of stitches lend themselves to these effects.

Leaf stitch is versatile and suitable for individual leaves and small-scale trees; it can be worked as an all-over pattern with the leaf shapes interlocking, or four can be stitched to form a star.

Petal stitch is a square-shaped stitch which can also be worked diagonally in diamond form. The circular weaving stitches raise the "petals" to give a flower-like effect.

Pinwheel stitch is an attractive variation of Milanese stitch (page 45), useful for large-scale flower heads. It can be used alone or in conjunction with other stitches.

Fantail stitch is similar to half a large circular eyelet, with additional stitches forming the "stem." It makes a useful all-over pattern of flower shapes.

Leaf stitch

To work in an upright position, begin with a vertical stitch over six horizontal threads. On each side of this, make three diagonal stitches, starting one thread down and one to the side, and inserting the needle below the vertical stitch. Working downward, make two more diagonal stitches of equal length on each side over three vertical and five horizontal threads.

▶ **Pauline Brown**
A detail of *Herbaceous Border* (see page 131) shows leaf stitch worked in various sizes with yarn as well as ribbon.

Leaf stitch variations

For an all-over pattern, the first rows of leaf stitches are worked side by side with subsequent rows interlocked. Sizes and shapes can be varied, and spaces can be filled with compensating tent stitches.

Leaf stitch star

This consists of four leaf stitches worked toward a central point. A long stitch can be added along the center of each leaf if required.

Diagonal leaf stitch

This is worked in a similar way to upright leaf stitch, starting with a diagonal stitch worked over four intersections. An all-over pattern can be built up, and a star-shaped version made with four leaves.

Petal stitch

When worked over ten threads of canvas, this square stitch has five stitches radiating from the center at each corner, in a similar way to the corners of eyelet stitch (page 46). The second part of the stitch, which can be worked in contrasting thread, involves winding the thread around the center hole several times, passing under the diagonal stitches.

Pinwheel stitch

This is worked in a similar way to Milanese stitch (page 45), but has four triangles meeting at a central point. Each of these is made with four diagonal stitches worked over one, two, three, and four intersections. Between these, four more triangles of four horizontal or vertical stitches are worked.

Fantail stitch

The semicircular "eyelet" is worked over ten vertical and five horizontal threads with fifteen stitches radiating from the center hole. The stem is made with straight and diagonal stitches which fill in the gaps when the stitch is worked as an all-over pattern.

Textured Stitches

An innovation in recent years has been the introduction of texture to complement the inherently smooth effect of needlepoint. This can be achieved in two ways.

Surface embroidery stitches can be worked, either following the mesh of the canvas or disregarding it by working over a previously stitched area. Some of the most popular stitches for this type of effect are bullion and French knots, chain and whipped chain (pages 30 and 17), but any other surface stitch can be used.

There are also a few needlepoint stitches which create texture, one being *velvet stitch*. It produces loops which can be cut to give a tufted pile and is useful for a wide range of subjects from fluffy animals to the centers of flowers.

Rhodes stitch, named after its creator, Mary Rhodes, is a versatile, bulky stitch worked over any number of threads. Large-scale versions can be secured in a similar way to crossed cushion (page 48), with diagonal stitches worked across the corners.

You can also embroider half a Rhodes stitch, in which case you will need other stitches such as tent (page 40) or straight stitches to fill in the gaps. For *half Rhodes half-drop*, subsequent rows interlock to form an overall pattern.

Norwich stitch, also known as waffle stitch, consists of a series of diagonal stitches worked in rotation to form an interwoven square. Both Rhodes and Norwich stitch lend themselves to bold geometric designs.

Norwich stitch

1 This is worked over a square with an uneven number of threads of canvas. Start with a cross stitch from corner to corner, then bring the needle out one thread up from the beginning, making a diagonal stitch alongside the first stitch.

2 Bring the needle out one thread to the right of the second stitch and make the next stitch alongside the second.

3 Continue working a series of parallel stitches around the square.

Rhodes stitch

Rhodes stitch variations

Velvet stitch

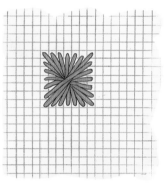

1 Begin with a diagonal stitch across the square; bring out the needle one thread to the right of where you began and insert it one thread to the left of, and crossing, the first diagonal stitch.

2 Continue working counter-clockwise around the square, crossing the previously worked stitches until the area is completed.

The corners of Rhodes stitch can be held down with diagonal stitches of the same or contrasting yarn. Half Rhodes stitches can be interspersed with tent stitch or upright Gobelin. Half Rhodes half-drop consists of rows of half Rhodes stitches worked side by side, with the second row encroaching halfway down the first.

Work a half cross stitch from bottom left to top right over one or two intersections of canvas. Repeat this stitch, leaving a loose loop, and hold it down with the thumb of the non-working hand. Then complete the other half of the holding cross stitch, going from bottom right to top left. The loop can either be left or cut to give the velvet-pile effect. Complete the bottom row first, and work toward the top of the area to be filled.

BARGELLO EMBROIDERY

Several theories exist as to the origins of Bargello work, also known as Florentine embroidery, flame stitch, and Hungarian point – one legend being that it was brought to Italy when a Medici nobleman married a Hungarian bride in the 15th century.

The distinctive repeating patterns of this type of needlepoint are all worked on single canvas with vertical stitches, usually in wool. Other types of yarn can be used, but bear in mind that straight stitches do not cover the canvas as thoroughly as diagonal ones.

This technique relies for much of its effect on the shading of the colors. The patterns fall into two main categories, those worked across the canvas in curved or zigzag rows, and motif or medallion designs. In both cases, all the stitches are the same length, except when embroidering Hungarian point designs, which consist of rows of long stitches interspersed with short ones.

Bargello embroidery is suitable both for decorative panels and a number of practical items such as pillows, chair seats, totes, and evening bags. In such cases, the stitches should be restricted to a fairly short length to avoid snagging.

Charting a design

Unless you are working experimentally with no formal pattern, line charts are used for Bargello embroidery – it is necessary to work only one row of the basic repeat pattern, which can then be stitched as many times as necessary across the canvas. Subsequent horizontal rows usually follow the contours of this foundation row exactly.

In the case of symmetrical motifs, only the top half needs to be charted, as the lower half is a mirror image – it is in fact helpful to use a mirror to establish the appearance of a motif.

Since Bargello embroidery is usually symmetrical, it is practical to begin in the center of a row, stitch to the right, and then return to the center prior to working the left-hand side. This allows you to refer across to the previously worked area in order to keep the stitches in line.

Bargello stitch

Generally worked vertically over an even number of threads, Bargello stitch resembles upright Gobelin (page 41). The most usual size is over four horizontal threads, with the next stitch dropping down two threads, but this can be varied to produce differing patterns.

▶ **Fiona Lewis**
This Bargello embroidery has used a random approach.

Zigzags and curves

The simplest Bargello zigzag design is produced with stitches of similar size, dropping down or extending up across the canvas in a regular manner. For a shallower zigzag, two or more stitches are worked at each level. Curves are made with two or three stitches worked in steps on the same level toward and at the top or bottom of a zigzag.

Motif (or medallion) designs

To establish a medallion, place two mirrors at right angles to each other on a charted design and slide them along until a suitable motif appears. Draw in the horizontal and vertical perimeters of the shape and re-draw, incorporating the mirrored design.

Hungarian point pattern

This is a spiky zigzag pattern made up of groups of both long and short vertical stitches alternating in the same row. The long stitches are usually over four or six threads, while the short are worked over two.

Pinnacle pattern

The pointed effects of pinnacle patterns are created with long stitches, usually over six threads. Each one drops down or extends up over five threads in steep steps.

▲ **Fiona Lewis**
Hungarian point pattern borders this needlepoint sampler.

FOUR-WAY BARGELLO

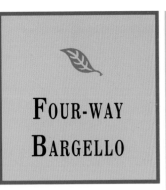

In this attractive variation of Bargello embroidery the pattern is stitched in each direction to form a radiating design of four identical triangles. Rows of curves and zigzags, or motifs can both be adapted to form this four-way modification.

As with normal Bargello work, the main structure of the design can be charted on graph paper, and if two mirrors are used to help formulate the design, only a quarter of it needs to be drawn. It is best to establish the design away from the center point. Subsequent rows of stitching can follow the shape exactly as you work toward the center and then outward to cover the surrounding area.

Compensating stitches (page 41) will be needed to complete the diagonal and the outer edges.

► **Joyce Robertson**
Four-way Bargello makes an attractive little cushion.

Preparing the canvas

Mark the canvas by drawing or basting two diagonal lines from corner to corner plus perpendicular lines across the center.

Stitching the design

To establish the pattern in the top quarter, start some way above the middle point and in the center of a row, stitching toward the right-hand diagonal line. Return to the center and complete the row to the left. Repeat this pattern in the other three directions. It may be necessary to make small compensating stitches where the quarters join. Work toward the center and then complete the surrounding area by repeating the first row and changing the color as necessary.

COUNTED THREAD EMBROIDERY

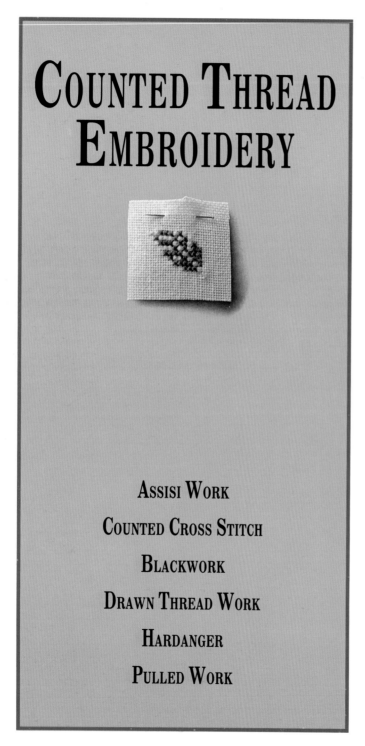

ASSISI WORK

COUNTED CROSS STITCH

BLACKWORK

DRAWN THREAD WORK

HARDANGER

PULLED WORK

Counted thread embroidery is a generic term for a number of techniques. In each technique, a stitch is worked over an exact number of threads, resulting in designs which tend to be precise and often geometric. Included in this category are counted cross stitch, Assisi work, pulled and drawn thread work, Hardanger, and blackwork.

Fabrics

All counted thread methods are stitched on evenweave fabric, which is woven with the same number of horizontal (weft) threads as the vertical (warp) threads. Specialist embroidery evenweaves are usually cotton or linen with a range of from 12 to 32 threads per inch. Some fabrics such as Aida and Hardanger are made with groups of threads woven together.

Needles

Tapestry needles (available in sizes 13–24) should always be used for counted thread methods. They have blunt points and large eyes and slip easily between the threads of the fabric without splitting the fibers.

Frames

Counted thread work should always be mounted in a frame. If a circular embroidery hoop is used, always make sure that the warp and weft are not distorted.

Box charts

These are used for designing cross stitch and Assisi work as well as for tent stitch needlepoint patterns. Each square on graph paper represents one stitch, with either symbols or colors defining different colored areas in the design.

Assisi Work

Originating in the Italian town of that name, the particular characteristic of Assisi work is that the motifs are enclosed with double running stitch, sometimes called Holbein stitch, or backstitch, usually in a dark thread. The entire background area is then covered with cross stitch in a contrasting medium shade. Additional details are sometimes added in double running stitch. Designs should be worked out on graph paper.

Fabric
Use evenly woven cotton, linen or wool, including embroidery evenweaves of either single or double thread construction. Unless the piece of embroidery is very small, it should be framed for working.

Threads
Coton à broder, stranded floss or pearl cotton, which is a similar thickness to or thinner than the weave of the background fabric, should be used.

Needles
Tapestry needles should be used.

Following a box chart

Box charts are drawn onto graph paper paper with each square representing a single stitch, such as a cross or a tent stitch. The squares are either filled in with the intended colors, or symbols representing the colors are used. This type of chart is normally used for counted cross stitch, Assisi work, and needlepoint designs worked entirely in tent stitch.

▶ **Pauline Brown**
This reversed repeat motif is taken from traditional peasant-style embroidery.

Double running stitch

Working from the box chart, it is usual to begin by stitching the outlines of the design in double running stitch. Make the outline of single running stitches each over two threads of fabric. Turn the work and on the return journey work another row of running stitches into the same holes, filling in the gaps left in the first line.

Cross stitch

Once the outlines are completed, cross stitch is used to cover the background areas, leaving the motif as a "negative" area. The cross stitch is worked as for counted cross stitch (page 42), over two threads of fabric, keeping the top thread of each stitch slanting in the same direction. You can work one stitch at a time or you can work all in one direction, then work back to complete the stitch.

COUNTED CROSS STITCH

This is one of the most familiar of embroidery techniques, relying for its effect on clearly defined designs and good choice of color. It is used in peasant embroidery in many parts of the world; in England counted cross stitch became popular for samplers in the 18th and 19th centuries.

Fabrics
Evenweave fabric in cotton or linen, with from 12 to 34 threads per inch is ideal. Usually cross stitch is worked over two threads, with the fabric's degree of fineness determining the size of the stitch. With fabrics such as Aida and Hardanger, which are woven with groups of threads forming the weave, it is usual to stitch over one intersection only. Small pieces of cross stitch can be worked in the hand, but it is advisable to use a hoop for larger-scale work.

Threads and needles
Choose a thread similar to or finer than the weave of the fabric. Stranded floss or silk and coton à broder produce clearly defined stitches. For larger-scale work, fine tapestry yarn or linen or crochet yarns can be used. Tapestry needles of suitable size should be used.

Designs
Counted cross stitch is a favorite method for producing alphabets and decorative borders featuring either flowers or abstract patterns. There are a large number of cross-stitch kits on the market, but it is more rewarding to produce individual designs using original drawings, photographs, or photocopies. Designs can be worked out using a box chart made by tracing the subject onto transparent graph paper.

Work out your design on graph paper, make any final adjustments and then use this as a guide for your embroidery.

Counted cross stitch

Though it is usual to work over two threads of fabric when stitching on evenweave linen, cross stitch can in fact be done over any number of threads.

Fine cross stitch can be used for monogramming household linens. Excellent commercial patterns are available.

On Aida or similar fabrics which have groups of threads woven in a type of basketweave, stitches are normally worked over a single intersection.

Starting and finishing cross stitch
This method can be used for all types of counted thread embroidery. Begin by leaving a short length of thread on the right side. After a few stitches, pull this to the back of the work, thread it in a needle and darn it into the back of three or four stitches. Finishing is done in the same way, with the thread darned through the back of the previously worked stitches.

▲ Border
An example of a border design

▶ Susan Smith
Mauve Valentine
Counted cross stitch is a useful medium for lettering and for detailed designs. Here it is combined with pulled work.

▼ ABC
An example of a cross-stitch alphabet.

BLACKWORK

Blackwork, sometimes known as Spanish blackwork, appears extensively on Tudor costume. It is thought to have been introduced to Britain by King Henry VIII's Spanish wife, Catherine of Aragon.

It is a counted thread method based on vertical, horizontal, and diagonal backstitches or running stitches, which form decorative geometric patterns.

Fabrics
Specialist embroidery evenweaves in cotton or linen with 22 to 26 threads per inch are the most suitable for traditional-style work, but any smooth-surfaced evenly woven fabric can be used for a freer approach. Framing the work will help to achieve good tension.

Threads and needles
This technique is usually worked in black thread – hence the name – sometimes with the addition of red or gold details. In contemporary work a limited palette of other colors is sometimes introduced.

Use tapestry needles, and smooth-textured threads such as coton à broder, stranded floss, or pearl cotton which are similar to or finer than the weave of the background fabric. Fine metallic threads or filament yarns are suitable for details.

Designs
Traditionally, designs have been based on geometric patterns filling the main areas which are outlined in backstitch – or for heavier lines in chain or stem stitches (page 16). These can be worked out on graph paper using a box chart (page 59). Freestyle designs which include a limited number of outlines and changes in density of stitch can be marked on the fabric with an erasable marker.

Backstitch

This is worked as for surface embroidery (page 14), but usually over two threads of fabric. For blackwork, the stitch can be worked horizontally, vertically, or diagonally, and as there is no recognized sequence of stitching, it is necessary to devise the most logical way of embroidering each individual pattern.

Algerian eye stitch

Starting at the top right-hand corner, work radiating stitches in a clockwise direction around a square consisting of four threads. The needle is taken down into the center hole for each stitch and brought up at the edge of the square.

Creating tone

Gradations of tone can be achieved in two main ways, the first being to use threads of varying thicknesses for the same stitch. The second method, when using an all-over geometric design, involves progressively omitting more and more of the pattern.

◄ **Blackwork**
Different types of blackwork pattern are shown here.

◄ **Amanda Ewing**
Two Dogs
The diminishing density of the pattern creates the form and shading of the animals.

DRAWN THREAD WORK

This type of embroidery is most often used for items of table linen. As its name indicates, the technique involves withdrawing threads from the background fabric to produce a delicate openwork effect. Either the warp or the weft threads are removed, and decorative stitches are then worked over the remaining threads, forming borders or bands.

The foundation of most drawn thread work is hemstitching. This is worked on each side of the band of withdrawn threads and holds groups of the remaining fabric threads together. Open corners are made by withdrawing bands of both warp and weft threads. These can be treated decoratively with needlewoven effects.

Fabrics

For table linen choose evenweave linen or cotton which is loosely woven enough for the threads to be withdrawn easily. Other fabrics such as furnishing sheers (a loosely woven fabric) or burlap could be used for less practical items such as wallhangings. Correct tension is achieved more easily if the work is framed.

Threads and needles

For traditional hemstitching use cotton or linen thread, choosing a color and texture that closely matches the background fabric. For a freer approach, any thread can be used. Work with tapestry needles of a suitable size.

Designs

Because of the nature of the technique, designs are mainly restricted to borders, squares, or rectangles. Bands of stitchery can also be worked either parallel or at right angles to each other. For a precise design which needs to be centered, mark the center with a line of basting, then baste along both edges of the areas to be withdrawn.

Preparation

Mark the center and baste precisely around the area where the threads are to be removed. With a small pair of embroidery scissors, carefully cut the horizontal threads at the center. Withdraw these using a tapestry needle and leaving the exact number of vertical threads required. Darn the withdrawn threads a short distance into the fabric at each end and trim off the excess.

Hemstitching

1 Darn the working thread between several vertical threads and bring the needle out two or three threads below the left-hand end of the open area.

2 Pick up three or four vertical threads and, encircling these, insert the needle to the right from the back, bringing it out again two threads below.

Ladder stitch

This consists of ordinary hemstitching worked on each side of a withdrawn band, so that the same group of threads is bound on each side.

Zigzag hemstitch

Work hemstitch along the lower edge of a withdrawn band, making sure that each group contains an even number of vertical threads. Then turn the work and hemstitch the other edge, grouping the threads so that half are taken from each adjacent group.

Double hemstitch

This is worked between two bands of withdrawn threads, with four to six threads of fabric left between them. Starting from the right, backstitch over three or four threads at the top of the lower withdrawn band. Then make a diagonal stitch on the back of the work, bring the needle out at the bottom of the top band, and make a backstitch over the same three or four threads. Repeat.

Interlaced hemstitch

Hemstitch both edges of a wide withdrawn band as for ladder stitch. For the interlacing, fasten the thread in the center of the right-hand end. Take the needle from left to right under the second group of threads, then over the first group. Bring the needle forward, twisting the groups of threads. Repeat.

Preparation

The open space which results when threads are withdrawn in both directions can be decorated in a variety of ways. Cut and withdraw two sets of threads, one group horizontally and the other vertically. Darn in the ends (page 64) and reinforce the two outer edges of the space with buttonhole stitch (page 20). Work the chosen hemstitching along both lengths of the withdrawn threads.

Spider's web corner

1 Make a cross stitch (page 42) across the open corner, fastening off firmly; overcast one diagonal stitch, and then overcast halfway along the other.

2 Work a spider's web (page 28) on this base of four stitches. Finish by completing the overcasting on the second diagonal stitch.

▲ **Sarah Cookson**
This sampler displays stitches of varying complexity and uses colored threads.

Woven corner

Needleweaving

1 This is particularly suitable for incorporating with interlaced hem stitching. Extend the threads used for the interlacing right to the edge of the open area and then make a cross stitch as for the woven corner to form a double cross stitch at the corner. Overcast one diagonal stitch, and then overcast half-way along the other.

2 Then start weaving as for woven wheels (page 28). Work a spider's web (page 28) on this base of eight stitches. Finish by completing the overcasting on the second diagonal stitch.

1 Groups of threads can be overcast or woven together either informally or in precise patterns. Overcasting consists of wrapping a group of threads in a withdrawn area with the working thread.

2 When weaving, groups of threads are darned back and forth. These can be pulled away from the perpendicular for an irregular effect, or patterns simulating woven motifs can be created.

HARDANGER

This type of openwork counted-thread embroidery takes its name from a mountainous district in Norway. It is characterized by rectangular groups of satin stitches known as "kloster blocks," which enclose the cut areas.

Remaining bars of warp or weft threads are usually needlewoven together, and open centers may be embroidered in a similar way to drawn thread work corners (pages 66–7). Additional satin stitch patterns such as stars are sometimes worked on the areas surrounding the kloster blocks.

Hardanger is most often used for table linen and embroidered in white or cream threads or threads which harmonize with the background fabric.

Fabrics
A specialist embroidery evenweave known as Hardanger fabric is used. Firmly woven with double threads, Hardanger fabric is available in a variety of colors.

Threads and needles
Choose a matching or harmonizing thread such as pearl cotton, which is of a similar weight to the Hardanger fabric. Use a tapestry needle of suitable size for the thread.

Designs
Hardanger designs are invariably geometric as it is difficult to work this technique freely. Kloster blocks can take the form of squares, diamonds, and triangles which are drawn on a line chart (page 39). Shade in the areas which are to be cut away.

▲ **Margaret Rivers**
An example of Hardanger shows kloster blocks with overcast and woven bars, together with loop stitch filling. Also included are spider's web corners (page 67).

Kloster blocks

Groups of horizontal and vertical satin stitches are worked to enclose areas which are subsequently cut away. The simplest form is a square consisting of groups of five stitches worked over four threads and placed at right angles to one another. A diamond block can be made with 12 similar groups of satin stitch.

Cutting and withdrawing threads

When the kloster blocks have been completed, parts of the area which they enclose are carefully withdrawn and cut away. This is done in a similar way to drawn thread work (page 64), but the ends are trimmed and not darned in. Only those threads which are at right angles to the ends of the satin stitches are cut away.

Woven and overcast bars

When groups of threads are withdrawn in a kloster block, a number of loose ones are left between areas of fabric. These are either needlewoven or overcast as for drawn thread work (page 64).

Loop stitch

Worked in the open square left by the withdrawn threads, a loosely tensioned buttonhole stitch is made through the middle stitch of each group of satin stitches.

Additional decoration

Satin stitch surface decoration can be worked around or adjoining the cut areas. Blocks, diamonds, stars, pyramids, and miters incorporate horizontal, vertical, or diagonal stitches.

PULLED WORK

Also known as pulled thread work and drawn fabric, this type of embroidery probably began as an imitation of lace, with texture and pattern being the most important features.

The technique differs from drawn thread embroidery (page 64) in that the openwork effect is achieved not by withdrawing threads, but by pulling some threads together and others apart.

Pulled work is suitable for table linen and can also be useful for combining with other techniques, such as surface stitchery, to add texture to otherwise undecorated backgrounds.

Fabrics

Although it is traditionally embroidered on evenweave linen with stitches carefully counted, it can also be worked in a more random fashion on loosely woven fabrics such as scrim or sheer furnishing fabric. Tension is an important aspect of pulled work, so the fabric should be framed before stitching.

Threads and needles

For conventional pulled work, choose a strong thread which matches the back-ground fabric – threads can be withdrawn from the background and used for the stitching. Coton à broder, button thread, crochet cotton, and pearl cotton are all suitable, used in a tapestry needle of suitable size.

Designs

While traditional designs are generally based on geometric forms, a more contemporary approach features random blocks of pulled-work patterns.

Either way, the design can be marked on the fabric with basting stitches or with an erasable marker.

▼ **Lydia Solomon**
A variety of pulled work stitches have been embroidered on a loosely woven fabric.

Tension

An important aspect of pulled work is the tension of the individual stitches. In most cases, the thread is pulled tightly, bringing the fabric threads together and creating patterns of holes.

For clarity, however, line charts usually depict the stitches with a slack tension as for other counted thread methods. The effects of different tensions are most easily seen when working satin stitch. If the thread is left untensioned (top), it appears as a wide band on the surface. If it is pulled tight (bottom), a row of holes appears on each side of the narrow band. Satin stitch is the basis for a range of fillings.

Chessboard filling

This consists of blocks of alternating vertical and horizontal satin stitches. Each block is composed of three rows of ten satin stitches worked over three fabric threads. Work the rows consecutively in the direction shown.

Small chessboard filling

A smaller version of chessboard filling can be worked in double rows consisting of seven stitches made over three threads. The thread in both chessboard fillings may be pulled tight or remain slack.

Step stitch

This is worked diagonally with blocks of five satin stitches made over four threads alternating in direction in a step formation. Start the first horizontal block at A, finishing at B; then work the first vertical block at C ending at D, and so on.

Single faggot stitch

This consists of a series of tensioned backstitches worked diagonally in steps, usually over four threads. Bring the needle out at top right at A, insert it four threads to the right at B. Then bring it out at C (four threads below A) and insert it again at A, before bringing it out four threads to the left of C at D. Repeat. For the second row, turn the work and repeat the stitch alongside the first row, using the adjacent holes made by the first row.

Wave stitch

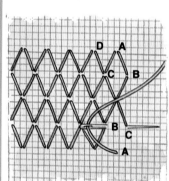

A series of tensioned diagonal backstitches are worked in horizontal lines over an even number of threads. Working from the right, bring the needle out at A, insert it at B diagonally four threads down and two to the right; then bring it out at C (four threads to the left). Insert it again at A and bring it out at D (four threads to the left). The second row is worked from the left.

Window filling

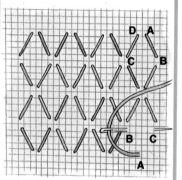

This variation of wave stitch is worked over an uneven number of threads, with one thread left between the stitches. Bring the needle up at A, insert it at B (four threads down and two to the right), bring it out at C (five threads to the left) and insert it at D (one thread to the left of A). One thread is left between each row. Again, the second row is worked from the left.

Eyelets

These are stitched in a similar way to those worked on canvas (page 46), with a series of stitches converging in the center hole, which can be enlarged with a stiletto. The thread can be pulled tight or left untensioned.

Diamond eyelets

This variation worked as for needlepoint (page 46) can be used as a filling stitch or stitched as individual diamond shapes. The thread may be pulled tight or left slack.

Single cross eyelets

These are worked in a similar way to conventional eyelets, but a single thread is left between each quarter of the eyelet.

Freestyle eyelets

Variations on eyelets can be made by altering the shape and moving the hole off-center. For some, the thread can be pulled tight, while for others it is left slack.

▶ **Kathryn Francis**
Colored threads create a different effect from that of the more traditional self-colored method in this pulled work.

METAL THREAD EMBROIDERY

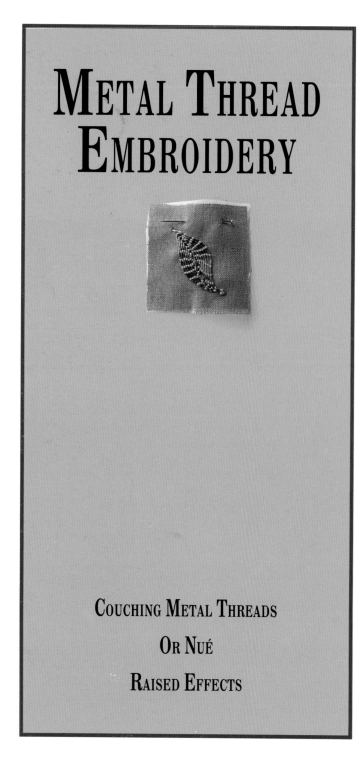

COUCHING METAL THREADS

OR NUÉ

RAISED EFFECTS

The great age of metal thread ecclesiastical embroidery, the "Opus Anglicanum" of the Middle Ages, is renowned throughout the world. Since then, gold and silver threads have been used whenever a sense of richness is desired for religious, ceremonial, or everyday purposes.

Metal thread (or goldwork) embroidery is regarded by many people as beyond their capabilities. However, it is really just a question of learning to manipulate the metal threads and working neatly on a small scale. The majority of the threads are laid on the background fabric and couched in place. Gold wires and plate can also be incorporated, as can beads and jewels.

Fabrics

Because of the weight of the threads, a closely woven fabric supported on a firm backing is required. Appliqué fabrics in silk, or small pieces of gold and silver kid, are often added, with felt and colored string used for padding. It is essential to frame the background fabric so that the surface is drum-tight.

Threads

Gold, silver, and copper threads come in a wide variety of qualities and types. Many are now processed in synthetic materials, which have the advantage of not tarnishing, but they lack rigidity and the esthetic qualities of those which contain real metal.

Jap gold, originally made with a paper-thin strip of beaten gold wound around a silk core, has a beautiful luster, while crinkle, twist, and various cords and braids can add texture to a design. Purls, which are tiny coils of metal cut into short lengths, are used as flexible beads.

For stitching metal threads in place, use a matching sewing silk or cotton thread.

Needles

Use fine crewel needles for couching, plus a large-eyed chenille needle for taking the metal threads through to the wrong side. Beading needles are required for attaching purls.

Designs

As with other types of surface embroidery, designs should be well planned. Couching of metal threads, although linear, can fill whole areas with richness and create a play of light on the surface. Texture can be achieved with the use of beads, purls, and padded areas. The design should be marked on the background fabric using a fabric marker.

COUCHING METAL THREADS

The principal technique used in metal thread embroidery is couching (page 77). Because of the rigidity of the threads, however, the methods used are not quite the same as those used for couching wool or silk. When applying *fine thread* or *cord*, two strands are usually couched simultaneously, giving a smooth line and covering the surface more quickly. *Braids* and *thicker cords* are stitched singly. While stitching, it is necessary to hold the metal thread taut. The ends are left on the surface until that area of the design has been completed and then taken through to the wrong side. *Pearl purl*, which is a rigid metal coil, and *plate*, a flat strip of metal, are treated differently in that they cannot be taken through to the wrong side of the background fabric.

Basic method

Position two strands of fine metal thread at the start of the stitching line, leaving the ends on the surface. Using a fine silk or cotton thread in a matching color, couch over both threads at ¼-inch intervals. To finish off the ends, thread each one separately into a chenille needle and pull it through to the back of the work. Overcast the ends on the wrong side.

Corners

To manipulate a stiff metal thread around a corner, insert the needle on the inner side of the outer thread and pull the thread around it so that it bends at a right angle. Couch the outer thread with a diagonal stitch. Repeat the bending and diagonal couching process with the inner thread. Continue the couching as usual.

Points

To turn a sharp point or corner, bend and couch the outer thread as for turning corners, with a diagonal stitch at the point. Cut the inner thread, take it through to the back of the work at the corner and secure it, then bring it back to the surface and restart it to dovetail alongside the outer thread. Continue couching both threads together.

Couching in a circle

In order to retain a smooth circular shape and outline, stagger the starting point of the double threads at the outer edge. Gradually work toward the center of the circle, couching at regular intervals so that the couching stitches converge in a pattern toward the center. Other shapes can be filled with couching in a similar manner.

Couching cords and braid

Heavy threads are usually couched singly, and care should be taken to prevent them from unraveling. A pair of pliers is useful for helping to take the thread through to the back of the work. Cords are couched with a diagonal stitch concealed between the twist of the cord. The end of the braid is taken through to the back of the material with a heavy needle. Flat braids are stitched with running stitches down the center.

Couching plate

Plate can be attached in straight lines or folded back and forth to form a zigzag pattern. To start and finish, fold back the ends and secure with a double stitch under the fold. For a crimped effect, lay a piece of plate along the length of a large-thread screw and press between the threads with your fingernail to form indentations in the plate.

Couching pearl purl

The effect of pearl purl can be varied by pulling out the coils to different thicknesses. It is couched in a similar way to cord, with an invisible diagonal stitch between the twists. In this case, the pearl purl is cut to the exact length required and the ends remain on the surface of the fabric, with a double stitch holding them firm.

OR NUÉ

Or nué, also known as shaded gold or Italian shading, is an ancient technique involving the couching of metal threads with fine colored threads to produce shaded patterns or images. The laid threads cover the entire surface of the design – or that of the area to be worked in or nué.

A smooth, shiny thread such as Jap gold is best and should be couched with a fine silk or cotton thread which will not cause the laid threads to part. The spacing of the couching stitches is varied to show different amounts of gold thread shining through. It is usual to couch the metal threads in straight lines across the design, which has been painted onto the background fabric. For a freestyle approach, experiments can be made with wavy lines or circular motifs incorporated into a goldwork design which uses other couching techniques.

Preparation
Transfer the design to the background fabric and color in the details with fabric paint. As with all types of metal thread embroidery, it is essential to frame the work as taut as possible.

▼ **Glenys Grimwood**
Larkspur
A contemporary or nué design has been worked in colored silks.

Couching

Pairs of metal threads are couched horizontally across the design, starting at the top left-hand corner. A gold-colored thread is used for couching the background, while colored threads chosen to match the colors in the design are used for the other areas. Couching is usually worked in a brick pattern, but the spacing of the stitches can vary, allowing you to achieve dense areas of color which will contrast with the shimmering effect of the gold showing between the couching stitches.

RAISED EFFECTS

Adding texture to an embroidery design always gives an extra dimension. In the case of metal thread embroidery, it can be achieved by padding and by the application of purls, beads (page 79), and jewels.

Sparkling metallic-effect fabrics can be stitched over a padding of *layers of felt*, as for other types of appliqué (page 88). Gold and silver kid, which is extremely lustrous and should only be used in small quantities, can also be padded with felt.

String which has been dyed yellow can be couched in lines or other patterns and used as a basis for the application of fine cords such as Jap gold.

Small pieces of thin, colored *cardboard* can also be stitched to the surface ready to be covered with lines of couched threads.

Purls come in several sizes and three different qualities: smooth, which is very shiny; rough, which is matte; and check, which is textured. They can be cut into lengths and stitched in a similar way to beads; and because they are flexible, they can be formed into loops or stitched over a padding of string.

Basket stitch couching

1 Lay a foundation of several lengths of yellow string, securing them to the background fabric with small stitches along the length and a double stitch at each end. The thickness of the string depends on the desired effect.

2 For the first row, start on the left, and couch pairs of threads at right angles to the foundation of string. Work a double couching stitch to the left of the first string, take the metal threads over two strings, and work a double stitch to the right of the second string. Repeat with a double stitch before the third string and after the fourth, and so on to the last string.

3 For the second row, repeat this couching method exactly so that four threads are laid together.

4 The third and fourth rows are couched in a similar way to rows one and two, but the thread is secured over one string only on the left-hand side, then couched over two strings as before, so that the flat areas alternate with the raised areas of the previous rows.

Padding with cardboard

To add texture to an otherwise flat area of couching, small shapes of cardboard or thick craft interfacing can be used as padding. Baste to the background and work horizontal lines of couched threads to cover them and the surrounding area, with the couching stitches forming an outline around the shape.

Attaching purls

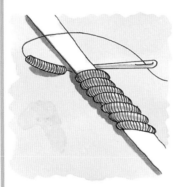

Couch a foundation length of string, securing it firmly at each end with a double stitch. Cut short lengths of purl, but long enough to cover the string at a slight angle. Use a beading needle and a fine thread which has been drawn through a block of beeswax to strengthen it. Stitch the pieces of purl diagonally over the string foundation.

Purls as beads and loops

Different types of purls can be cut into varying lengths and stitched to form patterns, textures, or decorative motifs. To make loops, a length of purl is threaded onto the beading needle and the needle taken through to the back close to where it originally emerged.

Jewels, beads, and sequins

Flat-backed colored glass jewels and stones are suitable for creating a focal point in a design. Some have holes through which they can be attached. Others can be held in place as for shisha glass (page 109), covered with a mesh of lurex or net, or encircled in a ring of leather.

▼ Pauline Brown
King's Head
A variety of threads and techniques are combined here with appliquéd fabric and leather, plus trapunto quilting to depict the face.

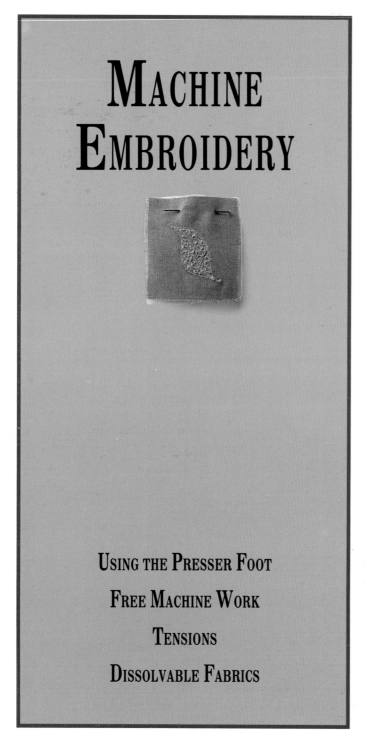

MACHINE EMBROIDERY

USING THE PRESSER FOOT

FREE MACHINE WORK

TENSIONS

DISSOLVABLE FABRICS

The sewing machine has come a long way since its invention in the 19th century – nowadays, automatic, electronic, and computerized machines provide a wealth of ready-made embroidery stitches and patterns.

The sewing machine can also, of course, be used as a replacement for hand stitching for techniques such as appliqué, quilting, cutwork, etc. In addition, creative and inventive free-style machine embroidery can be produced with an ordinary sewing machine, provided it has a drop-feed and zigzag facility.

It is essential to get to know the finer points of your sewing machine and master the ordinary stitching techniques – once you have done this, you can embark on creative work with confidence. Some techniques may require adjustment of the tension. For normal stitching, the top and bottom threads should be equally tensioned, producing an even stitch with the top and bottom threads linked precisely, but this is not always necessary for embroidery stitches.

Fabrics

For machine embroidery with the foot on, most types of fabric are suitable, although those which stretch easily need careful handling. For free machining (page 84), firm fabrics such as muslin or poplin are easiest for the beginner.

Stitching through an additional backing fabric, which acts as a support, will prevent puckering, particularly for light fabrics.

Threads

Most types of sewing thread can be used, but machine embroidery threads now include shaded and metallics, which greatly increase the possibilities. For additional texture, various types of cord, as well as knitting, crochet, and hand-embroidery threads, can be couched by machine.

Needles

Machine needles come in sizes from 120 (heavy) to 70 (very fine). American equivalent sizes are 20 (heavy) to 10 (very fine). The average sizes, 90 and 100, are best for embroidery. Also available are twin and triple needles for parallel lines, and hemstitch and double hemstitch needles.

Designs

The thin line which straight machine stitching produces gives a delicate spidery effect which can result in rather weak designs. However, the stitching can be built up, overlapped and massed to form close textures.

Some embroiderers like to work freehand without marking the design on the fabric. However, a few lightly marked guidelines will give you confidence to make a start.

If you prefer a more precise approach, the reversed design, drawn on thin tracing paper, can be basted to the back of the fabric and the main outlines stitched through the paper, which is then torn away.

Straight stitching

Thread the machine and insert the bobbin in the normal way. Using the standard or the embroidery presser foot, experiment with different types of thread and different stitch lengths. Work stitches in spaced or overlapping rows or mass lines of stitchery to cover the background surface.

Zigzag and satin stitches

By adjusting the stitch width dial, various widths of stitch can be achieved. This is used in conjunction with the stitch length dial. For example, a wide satin stitch requires the highest number stitch width and the lowest stitch length. Experiment with different widths and lengths.

Automatic stitches

Prepare the machine as for zigzag stitching with a wide stitch width and a low number stitch length. Select an automatic embroidery stitch, test on scrap fabric for effect and then proceed using a variety of decorative stitches in rows.

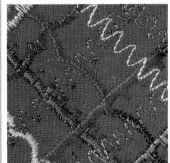

Experiment with different types of thread, and vary the length and width of the stitches.

◄ **Pauline Brown**
Automatic stitches in shaded threads, secure bands of colored satins.

USING THE PRESSER FOOT

The most important of the built-in functions of a modern sewing machine is the zigzag facility, which means you can produce automatic embroidery stitches as well as lines of satin stitch.

The range of effects can be extended by attaching different types of presser feet. Most sewing machines have, in addition to the one used for normal stitching, a number of presser feet as standard accessories, while others can be obtained. There are feet for appliqué and quilting; a braiding foot which enables you automatically to couch down braid, cords, and heavy yarns; the darning foot, which is for free-style machine work with the feed dog lowered; and a grooved pintucking foot used in combination with twin and triple needles. An interesting looped effect can be produced with the tailor-tacking attachment.

Using the machine with a presser foot attached means that the fabric is automatically fed through, restricting the stitching to straight or wavy lines unless the foot is continuously lifted and the work turned.

Hemstitch needles

Use fine, crisp fabrics such as organdy or other cotton. The single hemstitch needle pierces holes in the fabric. Set the stitch width to 2 and the length to 1.

The double needle uses two top threads and produces a line of straight or zigzag stitches plus the pierced holes. Set the stitch width to 0–2 and length 2. When working several rows, one needle normally pierces the holes in the previous row.

Twin and triple needles

Insert the needle and attach the appropriate pintucking foot to produce parallel lines of stitchery. For an Italian quilted or trapunto effect (page 103), thread a thick yarn through the stitching on the back of the work.

Tacking foot

Attach the tailor tacking foot and set the stitch width to 4 and the stitch length to 1. As the stitching proceeds, a line of loops is produced which slip off the foot, leaving a raised pile. Closely worked rows are effective if shaded thread is used.

Braiding foot

To couch cords, yarn, or heavy thread automatically onto the background fabric, attach the foot and thread the cord through the hole and under the foot. Set the stitch width to the same width as the cord and adjust the stitch length to your liking. Experiment with different cords, braids, and yarns and with some of the automatic embroidery stitches.

◀ **Pauline Brown**
This sample shows the use of various types of presser foot. The fluffy effect of the foliage is achieved with shaded thread and the tacking foot. The braiding foot is used to apply the cords in the foreground and for the wrapped cords of the bush. Twin-needle stitching creates the parallel lines of the field.

Wrapped cords

The braiding foot can also be used for wrapping threads and cords for additional decoration or finishing touches. Set up the machine as usual, but without a background fabric. Ease the cord through as the stitching proceeds, so that it is wrapped by the machine threads.

Textures and Patterns

Formal patterns and textures can be built up using automatic embroidery stitches.

For a more random approach the work has to be turned frequently and the stitch width altered.

Experimental stitches
Simple geometric and linear designs can be built up, and rows of stitches can be massed or overlapped to form areas of texture and color. As with all experimental work, practice is necessary, but there is much enjoyment to be had, particularly if you try out different fabrics and threads.

FREE MACHINE WORK

Free machine work, which is often compared to drawing with needle and thread, enables you to use the machine creatively.

There are two methods: one uses the darning foot, and the other is done by removing the presser foot completely. This means that the fabric is not fed automatically, but can be moved around by hand beneath the needle in any direction.

Both methods have their advantages, and it is up to individual embroiderers to decide which they prefer. In both cases the feed dog has to be disengaged. This is done by using the appropriate switch or button, or on older models, a cover plate is attached.

When free machining without the darning foot, it is essential to mount the fabric in a frame. Choose a shallow round wooden or metal embroidery hoop about 6 or 8 inches in diameter. It should have a screw for adjustment, and the inner ring must be bound with woven tape so that when the fabric is mounted, it is held firmly in place in both directions.

A bound frame is less likely to mark previously worked areas, should it be necessary to move to another part of the fabric. The inner ring should stand slightly above the other one so that the bottom surface comes directly into contact with the flat bed of the machine – the design will be uppermost on the inside of the ring.

If you prefer not to use a frame, you can work in a similar way by attaching a darning foot and lowering the feed and presser bar. Although it is a little more difficult to see exactly where the needle is piercing the fabric, this method has the advantage of allowing you to embroider larger areas without the need to move a frame.

Stitching

The machine is threaded in the normal way and the bobbin inserted. Whether you are using a darning foot or a frame, the length of the stitch is determined by how fast or slow the work is moved under the needle.

Machine embroidery with straight stitching tends to look thin and tentative unless the stitches are worked close together or overlapped to build up texture and form. If the machine is set to zigzag, the effect will be a wider line which will cover the ground more quickly.

Tensions

Most modern machines have an automatic tension adjustment for ordinary stitching, but it is necessary to alter the normal tension for some decorative effects and when using different types of thread either on top or in the bobbin.

The top tension is usually numbered on a dial at the front of the machine, which is simply moved to make an adjustment; the bottom tension can be changed by gently turning the screw on the bobbin case. This should be done very carefully so the screw does not become detached completely.

In each case, a certain amount of experimentation will be needed to get the correct relationship between the top and bottom tensions. For experiments, use contrasting colors of the intended weight for top and bobbin threads, as this will enable you to check the tension.

Using a frame

Disengage the feed dog and set the stitch width and length to 0. Remove the presser foot and position the dressed frame. Lower the presser bar and bring both threads to the surface of the fabric. These are trimmed when several stitches have been worked. Rest your fingers on the edge of the frame and begin to stitch, maintaining a fairly fast speed while moving the frame smoothly in any direction.

Using a darning foot

Attach the darning foot, and set up the machine as for free machine work with a frame. Do not forget to lower the feed dog. Stitch in the usual way, moving the fabric back and forth to create the design.

Free zigzag

Set the stitch width to 4 and work free machine embroidery as for straight stitching. Satin stitch dots can be worked by zigzagging on the spot.

Whip stitch

This produces a corded line with the lower thread whipping and completely covering the top thread. Use a firm sewing thread on top and a fine machine embroidery thread in the bobbin. Tighten the top tension and adjust the bottom tension only if necessary. Stitch quickly and move the frame slowly.

Cable stitch

A thick texture using threads such as pearl cotton, knitting yarn, or hand embroidery threads can be achieved by working on the reverse side of the fabric. The thick thread is wound by hand onto the bobbin and a thinner one used on top. Loosen the bottom tension so that the thread runs fairly smoothly and adjust the top tension if necessary.

◀ **Pamela Rooke**
Appliqué and free machine work make an effective combination in this underwater scene.

DISSOLVABLE FABRICS

In recent years, the production of "vanishing" fabrics has facilitated a technique which simulates lace and can be used as a fabric for garments or accessories. It is worked using free straight stitch machine work.

Originally, vanishing muslin and acetone were used for this type of lacy construction, but these have now been superseded by hot- and cold-water dissolvable fabrics.

Whole structures or areas of lacy fabric can be made for wallhangings and other decorative pieces, while lacy edgings and inserts can be fashioned by basting a fabric onto the dissolvable fabric and stitching heavily along and over the edge.

The method is also suitable for freestanding motifs such as flowers and butterflies. These can be molded into shape before they are dried, and then either stitched to a background or used on their own as three-dimensional pieces.

Pretty, delicate effects can be achieved with metallic and shaded threads, which can be placed either on top or in the bobbin.

Hot water dissolvable fabric is a fine-woven, pale blue material which can easily be stretched in a frame. When the embroidery has been completed, it is placed in a pot of boiling water for a few minutes, which causes the fabric to shrivel up and dissolve. To dry and re-shape the lace, it should be pinned out on a towel. Alternatively, it can be basted to a piece of muslin before immersion.

Cold water dissolvable fabric resembles a soft, white stretchy plastic. It dissolves very easily in cold water, and it does not shrivel up in the same way as the hot-water type. Its only drawback is that it tends to tear. Should this happen, an additional piece of the fabric can be placed beneath the hole.

◄ **Pamela Rooke**
Irises
Machine lace flowers have been embroidered on fabric that is dissolvable in cold water. Fine wire holds the petals in shape.

Outlining the design

Set up the machine for free machining (page 84) with the stitch length and width set to 0. Use machine embroidery thread throughout. Trace the design onto the dissolvable fabric and mount it in a frame. Work free machine embroidery over the outlines of the design several times, making sure that the lines overlap and interweave to make the lace hold together.

Filling in the design

To make a pattern within the shape, build up a network of lines which interconnect with each other and the outlines. Machine stitch each line several times, overlapping as for the outline. For a solid effect, the whole shape needs to be filled in with stitches worked in several directions.

Dissolving hot-water fabric

When the stitchery is complete, cut away as much of the dissolvable fabric as

possible before immersing it for a few minutes in a pan of gently simmering water. Rinse under warm running water.

Dissolving cold-water fabric

Cut away the excess fabric as previously, before plunging the embroidery into cold water.

Stretching and drying

Lay the lace on a towel to dry. If it has become distorted, stretch and reshape it, and if necessary pin it in place to dry.

Molding

For three-dimensional pieces, the lace can be pulled and molded into shape. This is made easier if it is only immersed for a short time so that some of the dissolvable fabric is left between the machine stitching. For added stiffness, spray-on starch or shade stiffener can be used.

The basis of appliqué is the stitching of cutout designs of different fabrics to a background to create a decorative effect. The method can be used for anything from a simple motif on a bag or T-shirt to a fabric picture, or a full-scale quilt. Falling into the same category as appliqué would be highly textured wallhangings or even three-dimensional forms which use fabrics creatively.

One of the advantages of appliqué is that it is relatively quick to do. Although in the past it was worked by hand, nowadays many people prefer to use the sewing machine for speedy results.

The traditional methods of applying bold shapes to a background are now often adapted, extended, or modified, with padded and three-dimensional effects being very popular. Transparent fabrics come into their own in shadow appliqué, and even paper and plastic are sometimes featured in contemporary work.

Appliqué can also be used in combination with other embroidery techniques, particularly quilting and surface stitchery, which help to bring out the design in different ways.

Fabrics
Almost any fabric is suitable for appliqué – your choice will depend on the project's use as well as its visual impact. Fabrics such as felt and leather, which do not fray, can be applied direct without turn allowances. Those which do fray, such as silk, linen, synthetics, and cotton, are usually stitched with a turned edge, although today's embroiderers sometimes prefer to exploit the qualities of raw edges, or use a fusible web to apply the fabrics direct.

Although appliqué pieces were not backed in the past, iron-on interfacings and fusible web are often used and are suitable for some methods. For hand appliqué, it is advisable to frame the background fabric.

Needles
Any embroidery needle which suits the appliqué fabric can be used. Leather needles are useful for applying leather and plastic, and circular needles can be used for some three-dimensional work.

Designs
In general terms, designs for appliqué are usually fairly bold – often the shapes are simplified, which makes appliqué an ideal method for children's wear or sportswear. A more sophisticated approach, however, might include more intricate shapes which can be applied with fusible web. Subject matter can be realistic or abstract, with color and texture being stressed.

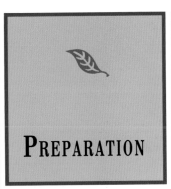

PREPARATION

Each appliqué technique requires preparation, and the cutting out and positioning of the fabric pieces must be planned with care. If a design has been drawn up to the correct size, it can be traced to make a paper template for each piece. Sometimes the complete design is drawn onto or transferred to the background fabric ready for the appropriate appliqué pieces to be stitched in place, but this is not always necessary – the cutout shapes can often be positioned by eye, using the drawn design as a guide.

If a design is to be placed centrally, the center of both the design and the background fabric should be determined by folding them into quarters and marking the horizontal and vertical lines which are then aligned when the design is placed on the fabric ready for transferring or as the appliqué motif is being positioned.

Preparing paper templates

Make a tracing of the design on tracing paper, numbering each shape if necessary. Mark the vertical alignment of each piece with an arrow, so that you can cut each shape on the straight grain of the fabric. Cut out each shape, ready to use according to the chosen appliqué method (i.e. with or without seam allowances).

Order of assembly

The prepared appliqué shapes must be applied in a logical order, overlappng as necessary. Start with the background and gradually superimpose the foreground pieces. It is usually better to overlap shapes rather than try to insert intricate pieces.

▼ **Rose Verney**
A hand-stitched appliquéd pillow uses the turned-edge method. The edge is secured with running stitch.

INTERFACING

In traditional appliqué methods, interfacings were of course not used, but many modern embroiderers find them invaluable for some types of appliqué.

Iron-on interfacing, available in a wide range of thicknesses and qualities, is useful for turned-edge appliqué. It not only adds weight and body to the fabric pieces, but also helps to determine their finished size and shape. A bold, stiff effect can be achieved by using heavy craft interfacing, while a softer treatment might involve jersey or flimsy fabrics backed with a lighter-weight interfacing.

Fusible web, which is a paper-backed double-sided adhesive web, can be used for machine appliqué (page 96), Persian appliqué (page 99), and for intricately shaped pieces which could otherwise not be used. It gives an immaculate result with most fabrics and can also be used to bond different materials together. These can then be cut out and used as freestanding motifs.

Interfacing: preparation

Place the interfacing adhesive side up over the design and trace with a hard pencil or fabric marker. Mark the grain line and the pattern number on the nonadhesive side. Cut out the shape carefully and place it adhesive side down on the reverse side of the fabric, aligning the grain if necessary. Press with a steam iron set to the correct heat setting for the fabric.

Interfacing: cutting out

For turned-edge appliqué, cut around the shape, leaving a seam or turn allowance of between ¼ and ½ inch, depending on the size and shape of the pieces and the type of fabric. Turn the seam allowances over the edge of the interfacing and baste them in place.

If the interfacing is being used simply to strengthen the fabric for raw-edge appliqué, cut out the shape without seam allowances.

Interfacing: appliqué

Pin and baste the prepared appliqué in place on the background fabric and stitch in place (see pages 92–3).

Fusible web: preparation

Position the fusible web smooth (nonadhesive) side up over the reverse side of the design tracing. If you are using a template, place it with the wrong side up on the smooth side of the fusible web. Trace the outline, making a reverse image of the pattern piece. Mark the grain line and pattern number on the smooth side.

Cut out the shape, allowing a margin all around. Position this adhesive side down on the reverse side of the fabric, matching grain lines if necessary, and press with an iron set to the appropriate heat setting.

Fusible web: cutting out

Cut out the shape on the marked lines through both the backing paper and the fabric.

Fusing the appliqué

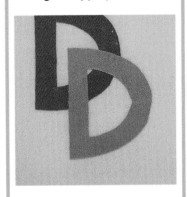

Peel off the backing and iron the shape in place onto the background fabric.

▼ **Anna Christy**
Indian Bedspread and Bird Still Life (detail)
Hand-colored silk and muslin has been stitched with raw edges showing.

TURNED-EDGE APPLIQUÉ

This is the best known of all hand appliqué methods, generally used for appliqué quilts, for fabrics which fray, and for padded appliqué. The pieces are cut out with a seam allowance and if desired can be backed with interfacing cut to the finished size. The seam allowances are then turned under and basted down, and the prepared shapes are stitched to the background, which can be done in a variety of different ways.

Slip stitch is unobtrusive, particularly if you use thread that matches the appliqué fabric. Stab stitch is more decorative and can be worked to give an evenly spaced dotted line. Buttonhole stitch (page 20) is also decorative, but may become overbearing. Use it with discretion, making tiny stitches which do not impose themselves too much on the design. A variety of other surface stitches can be used either to soften or accentuate the outline.

Marking and cutting out

If you are using iron-on interfacing (see page 90), iron it onto the reverse side of the fabric before cutting out. If not, mark the shape on the back of the fabric by drawing around a template or pin the cut-out tracing right side down on the back of the fabric. Cut along the drawn line or around the tracing, leaving a seam allowance of between ¼ and ½ inch.

Preparation

Fold under the seam allowance to the reverse side; clip, notch, or trim the allowances as necessary and stitch them down.

Stitching

Frame the background fabric on which the design has been marked. Pin and baste the prepared shape in place, smoothing any folds.

Slipstitch along the edge by bringing the needle up through the background fabric close to the edge of the motif and taking a tiny stitch into the turned edge. Remove the basting stitches.

Decorative stitches

Cretan, feather, and buttonhole stitch are all suitable for embellishing and covering the edges of applied fabrics.

Curves

If interfacing is not being used, it may be helpful to machine-stitch a line of staystitching on the fold line. For inward curves, clip the seam allowance at regular intervals to within ⅛ inch of the interfacing or staystitching. For outward curves, remove small notches of fabric from the seam allowance to reduce the excess bulk. Clip to within ⅛ inch as for inward curves. Fold over the seam allowance and baste it in place.

Points and corners

At outer corners and acute angles, trim the seam allowance to reduce bulk. Fold down the point first, then the two sides. On inner corners, clip the fabric up to the staystitching or the inter-facing and turn the sides under. Baste in place ready for attaching.

RAW-EDGE APPLIQUÉ

Nonwoven fabrics such as felt, net, and leather can all be cut out and applied directly without a seam allowance, either by machine or with stab or slip stitch.

Experimental decorative panels often include fabrics which have been cut out and randomly applied, with the raw edges creating a design feature. For a textured or impressionistic effect, tiny pieces of a variety of materials can be basted or glued in position prior to stitching by hand or machine.

▲ **Jill Cotton**
Letter S
Some pieces of this felt appliqué are overlaid with net.

PADDED APPLIQUÉ

Appliqué can be used in combination with a variety of different padding materials to create textured and raised areas. If the appliqué is non-woven, such as felt or leather, it is applied with raw edges on top of the padding, but for most other types of fabric the turned-edge method must be used.

The kind of padding you use depends both on the use to which the article will be put and on the effect you are seeking. Traditionally, layers of felt were used. They are particularly suitable for padding suede and leather or for areas of a design where firmness is needed. Synthetic batting produces a softer effect and allows you to work embroidery through it on the raised area. Cardboard or craft interfacing gives a stiffer, more precise result and is ideal for hard-edged subjects such as architectural or geometric designs.

Padding with felt

Cut out a piece of felt the same size and shape as the appliqué motif, then cut several more shapes, each slightly smaller than the previous one.

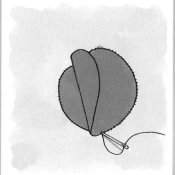

Starting with the smallest, pin and stitch it in the center of the area to be padded, using a stab stitch worked at right angles to the edge of the felt. Stitch the next size on top and repeat until each piece is attached, then sew down the prepared appliqué shape.

Padding with batting

Cut a piece of batting the same shape and size as the prepared appliqué shape. Stitch the batting to the background with loose straight stitches at right angles to the edge. Stitch the appliqué shape on top.

Cardboard or interfacing

Cut the cardboard or stiff interfacing to the size and shape of the finished appliqué. Cut out the fabric with a seam allowance. Center the cardboard on the reverse side of the fabric and apply fabric glue sparingly. Fold the fabric over the edge. Alternatively, use fusible web, ironing the seam allowance over the edge. Slipstitch the appliqué to the background.

THREE-DIMENSIONAL APPLIQUÉ

A popular method today, taking the theme of padded appliqué a step further, is the production of small free-standing motifs such as leaves and flowers, which are then stitched in place on embroidered or appliqué panels, boxes, or even garments.

Flat, raw-edged shapes can be made with two layers of fabric bonded together. If the motif needs to be manipulated into shape, florists' wire can be placed between the fabrics before bonding. A stiffened effect can be achieved by spraying with window-shade stiffener or applying a weak solution of fabric adhesive.

Padded shapes, with either raw or turned edges, can be stuffed with batting, and the edges and details embroidered either by hand or machine.

Flat bonded motifs

Using fusible web, fuse two fabrics together with the right sides out. Mark the design and cut out. The edges can be left unadorned, or decorative stitches and details can be added.

Padded raw-edged motifs

Mark the shape on the top fabric. Place it on the bottom fabric with a layer of batting between. Baste the layers together lightly and machine stitch (or backstitch by hand) along the marked outline. Cut out the motif close to the stitching and work machine satin or zigzag (or close buttonhole by hand).

Turned-edge motifs

1 Mark the shape on the reverse side of the top fabric. Place the top and bottom fabrics right sides together with the batting beneath. Baste them together, then machine stitch along the marked outline. Cut a diagonal slit in the bottom fabric. This will be used for turning the work. Remove the basting, cut out the motif, and trim the batting fairly close to the stitching.

2 Turn the motif right side out. Press lightly and stitch up the opening. Finish by topstitching the edge and details by machine, or add decorative edging by hand.

MACHINE APPLIQUÉ

Machine appliqué has the advantage of speed as well as producing an immaculate effect. It stands up well to hard wear or frequent washing.

In machine appliqué, the edges are usually crisply defined, and satin stitch is often used to make a bold outline. A sewing machine which has the facility for zigzag stitching is useful – some have a special transparent appliqué foot which enables you to see exactly where the needle pierces the fabric.

Although straight stitching can be used in conjunction with turned-edge appliqué, it is most usual to apply fabrics with raw edges. These can either be fused or basted in place, and the edges are then concealed beneath an outline of zigzag or satin stitch. The stitch-and-cut method is good for small pieces of appliqué. Automatic machine embroidery stitches give a decorative effect ideal for simple shapes, but for a less formal approach, free machine work can soften edges or produce additional color, texture, or pattern around a motif.

Fuse and stitch

Fuse the appliqué motif to the background fabric using fusible web (page 90). Put the appliqué presser foot on the sewing machine, set the stitch width and length to your chosen setting, and cover the edges with stitching.

Stitch and cut

Mark and cut out the motif to be applied, leaving a margin all around. Pin (and baste if necessary) in place on the background fabric, making sure that both fabrics lie smoothly.

Work straight machine stitches around the marked outline and then carefully cut away the excess fabric. If you wish, the edge can be covered with zigzag, satin, or decorative embroidery stitches.

Zigzag and satin stitch

Keeping the appliqué to the left of the needle, stitch in a clockwise direction around the motif so that the right-hand edge of the zigzag pierces the background fabric.

Zigzagging outside corners

Work zigzag or satin stitch to the corner, stopping the machine with the needle on the right. Keep the needle in the fabric and pivot the work, continuing stitching along the next side.

Zigzagging inside corners
Work in a similar way as for outside corners, but stop the machine with the needle to the left. Pivot and continue stitching.

Sharp points and corners

The zigzag stitch can be tapered by gradually narrowing the stitch toward the corner. Pivot the work as usual and stitch the other side, gradually increasing the stitch width.

Free machine work

Fuse or baste the appliqué motif in place. Mount the work in a frame and work free straight or zigzag machining (page 81) over the edges.

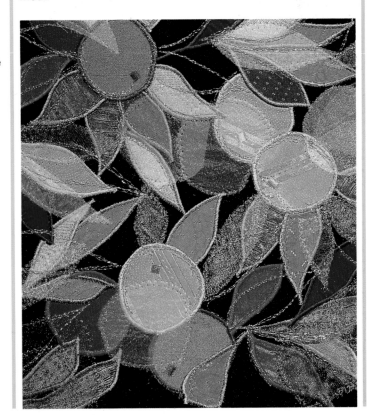

▶ **Greta Fitchett**
Apples
Silk, satins, and sheer fabrics have been appliquéd with satin and zigzag stitching.

SHADOW APPLIQUÉ

The delicate effect of transparent fabrics such as organdy, organza, and voile, used in a variation of the stitch-and-cut method (page 96), produces the technique known as shadow appliqué. In this case, the fabric to be applied is placed beneath the transparent background fabric, to provide the "shadow," and the excess is cut away after stitching.

Originally a hand method, sewn with pin stitch, shadow appliqué is now usually worked by machine using a narrow zigzag stitch. Traditionally, only white fabrics were used, both for the appliqué and the main fabric, but it is possible to experiment with different types of colored fabric.

The soft effects which are a feature of this technique make it a suitable medium for lingerie or evening wear. Designs should be fairly simple in concept, with clearly defined areas, rather like a stencil, so that the excess fabric can be easily removed.

Preparation

Trace the design onto the transparent fabric. For the appliqué, cut enough fabric to cover the whole design area and baste it onto the underside of the top fabric, making sure that the grains of both fabrics are aligned.

Katharine Guerrier
Here, colored fabrics have been used for the "shadows" and ornamental chain-stitched detail added through both layers.

Machine stitching

Work straight machine stitching along the marked outline and carefully cut away the excess fabric from the back layer of the work only. Finish by covering the edges of the appliqué with zigzag, satin, or free machine stitching.

Hand stitching

On the right side, work pin stitch through both layers before cutting away the excess fabric from underneath. To work pin stitch, work a backstitch from A to B along the marked outline and bring the needle up again at A. Repeat the backstitch on top of the first, bringing the needle up at C, inserting it again at A, and bringing it up at D. Pull the thread fairly tight to produce small holes in the transparent fabric.

PERSIAN APPLIQUÉ

Persian appliqué, also known as broderie perse, appliqué perse, and cretonne appliqué, developed in the 19th century as an inexpensive imitation of embroidery. Motifs such as birds, flowers, and animals were cut from printed cretonnes or other fabrics and reassembled on plain-colored backgrounds.

The pieces are applied with raw edges, and the simplest method is to iron a piece of fusible web to the back of the printed fabric before the motifs are cut out. When they have been positioned and ironed in place, they can be stitched by hand, either with invisible or decorative stitches, or with fancy or zigzag machine stitching.

This is a simple method particularly well suited to the inexperienced designer, as different arrangements of the cut-out shapes can be tried out on the background fabric before ironing down. It is ideal for pillows, quilts, and garments, where a quick and easy method is required.

Preparation

Cut out printed motifs with small sharp scissors. If you are using fusible web, this should be ironed on before the motifs are cut out.

Stitching

Arrange the cut-out motifs to form a satisfactory design and either fuse or pin and baste them in place on the background fabric. If working by hand, mount the work in a frame. Secure the edges with invisible slipstitches (page 92) or decorative hand stitches such as buttonhole stitch. Alternatively, machine stitch with zigzag, satin, or automatic embroidery stitches.

Katharine Guerrier
These flowers have machine-stitched detail added to the basic outline using shaded thread for a more subtle effect.

QUILTING

PADDED QUILTING

TRAPUNTO QUILTING

ITALIAN QUILTING

SHADOW QUILTING

MACHINE QUILTING

The origins of quilting are lost in history, but it is known that by the 16th century, padded garments were in common use as protection under armor, and silk quilts are often mentioned in the household inventories of the great European estates.

During the past hundred years, the popularity of quilting has increased in Europe and North America, not only for traditional quilts but also for garments, household items, and wallhangings.

There are several different quilting techniques, giving very different finished effects. All of them are relatively simple to do and can be stitched either by hand or by machine.

▼ Sonja Galsworthy
Tree forms
Beads have been added to this piece of padded quilting worked on satin.

Frames
It is advisable to use a frame for most types of hand quilting. The hoops used for quilting, deeper than the normal embroidery hoops, are available in a range of sizes, and are either circular or oval. Large floor-standing models similar to scroll or tapestry frames are used by professional quiltmakers, but these take up a great deal of space.

Marking the design
This should be done as lightly as possible, and several methods are suitable, including direct tracing (page 10) pricking and pouncing (page 10) or using stencils or templates (page 89).

Stitches for quilting
Backstitch (page 16).
Running stitch (page 15).

PADDED QUILTING

Padded quilting (also known as English quilting) consists of three layers – fabric, batting, and fabric – basted and stitched together either by hand or machine.

The Japanese technique of Sashiko, with its dark blue fabric and white hand stitching, is constructed in a similar way.

Fabrics
The top fabric may be any closely woven material, such as cotton, silk, or synthetic fibers. The choice of backing fabric depends on whether it will be seen, as it would be on a quilt, or hidden, as on a pillow cover. Synthetic batting can be washed or dry-cleaned and so is most often used, but silk, wool, and cotton batting (available from specialist quilting shops) give quilting a different character.

Threads
Strong quilting or buttonhole thread gives a clearly defined line.

Needles
Quilting needles (or betweens) are good, but any sharp embroidery needle of suitable size can be used.

Templates and stencils

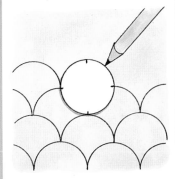

1 Using either templates or stencils to mark out repeat designs not only makes this process easier, but is more likely to be accurate. You can either cut your own stencil or template from cardboard or use a purchased one. On templates, either cut out notches or make marks at various points along the edges to make it easier to match the various parts of the design so that overlapping areas are uniform.

2 Quilting stencils have slits through which the design is marked. This results in broken lines that have to be joined when the stencil is removed. Use a quilter's marker, water-soluble pen, or dressmakers' chalk pen, pressing very lightly.

Basting

Having transferred the design to the top fabric, place it on top of the batting, which you have aligned carefully with the edges of the backing fabric. Check that the grain lines of top and backing fabric match. Pin the three layers together, smoothing out wrinkles from the center. Baste in grid formation, about 2 inches apart, starting at the center and working outward. Now mount the work in a frame (see page 100).

Stitching

To start a thread, make a small knot at the end, bring the needle up through to the right side, and tug gently to pull the knot through the backing fabric and into the batting but no further. To fasten off, take the thread through the batting a short way, bring the needle out through the backing fabric, and cut off the thread close to the surface.

When stitching the design, work small, even running stitches along the marked lines, through all three layers. For a solid line, backstitch can be worked, while embroidery stitches such as chain or stem stitch are sometimes used for a decorative effect. When quilting is used in combination with appliqué, the stitches are either made along the edge of the applied motif or a short distance from it, following the shape exactly.

TRAPUNTO QUILTING

Also known as stuffed quilting, this is a decorative method in which the small padded areas stand out in relief against a flat background.

Two layers of fabric are first basted together, then the motifs to be padded are enclosed with stitching so that they can be stuffed from the reverse side.

Fabrics
The top fabric needs to be pliable to accommodate the stuffing, while the backing should be lightweight but firm. Batting is usually used to stuff the motifs.

Threads
For decorative work, any embroidery or sewing thread may be used.

Needles
Embroidery needles of suitable sizes are best.

Preparation

Mark the design on the top fabric as for padded quilting (page 101). Pin and baste the top and backing fabrics together, matching grain lines, and mount the work in a frame (page 100).

Stitching

Work backstitch along the outlines of the design so that the motifs to be stuffed are enclosed. Close running stitch can be used if you prefer.

Stuffing

Keeping the work in the frame, turn it over to the wrong side. Taking care not to cut the top fabric, cut a small slit diagonally in the backing fabric within the outline of a shape that is to be stuffed. Insert small pieces of batting through the slit into the shape. Gently push the batting into any corners using a blunt implement, such as a knitting or tapestry needle. Check the front of the quilting – you should aim for a smooth, rounded shape – then carefully overcast the edges of the slit together.

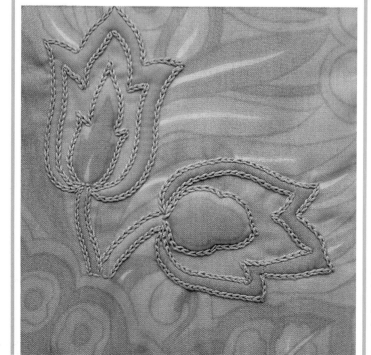

◄ **Pauline Brown**
Printed fabric has been raised to produce a relief effect with trapunto quilting for the main areas and Italian quilting for the outlines. As an alternative to backstitch, chain stitch has been used for a more decorative effect.

ITALIAN QUILTING

Like trapunto quilting, this method starts with two layers of fabric, but, in this case, double lines of stitching are worked. Then quilting wool, threaded in a large-eyed blunt needle, is inserted from the back of the work and run between the two layers of fabric and between the lines of stitching.

Fabrics
The top fabric should not be too stiff; otherwise, the quilting will not show up well. The backing fabric needs to be lightweight but firm.

Threads
The surface stitching is worked in sewing thread in a color that matches the background fabric. Quilting wool is used to fill the channels.

Needles
Embroidery needles of suitable sizes are ideal, while a large-eyed yarn needle is necessary for inserting the quilting wool.

Preparation

Mark the design on the top fabric as for padded quilting (page 101). Pin and baste the top and backing fabrics together, matching grain lines, and mount the work in a frame (page 100).

Stitching

Work parallel lines of backstitch or close running stitch along the marked lines.

▶ **Alison Collie**
Letter A
An interlaced design worked in Italian quilting is combined with a letter worked in padded trapunto quilting.

Insertion

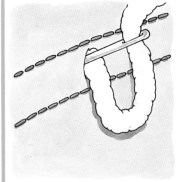

Loosen the tension of the work in the frame just enough to make the surface pliable. Thread the quilting wool into a large-eyed tapestry or yarn needle and insert it, from the wrong side, at the beginning of one of the channels and carefully turn it so it is lying between the parallel lines of stitching, pointing along the channels. Slide the needle carefully along the channel and bring it out again through the backing fabric. Re-insert the needle through the same hole to work the next part of the design. To avoid puckering at corners or sharp curves, leave the wool loosely tensioned. Keep a small pair of pliers at hand to pull the needle through.

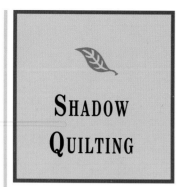

SHADOW QUILTING

There are several forms of this attractive method of quilting, but essentially it relies for its effect on the transparent top fabric used in its construction.

The most usual method is for a visible filling, such as colored felt shapes, to be basted between the top fabric and the backing, so that the raised shape shows through but is softened and diffused by the top fabric.

Shadow Italian quilting is worked in exactly the same way as Italian quilting (page 103), but the colors of the wools inserted in the channels show as delicate shadowy lines through the transparent top layer of fabric.

Trapunto quilting can also be adapted in this way by stuffing areas with strong colored batting or wool.

Fabrics

Shadow quilting relies for its effect on careful choice of fabrics and materials. The backing fabric and inserted materials should be strongly colored, while pale fabrics in organza, net, or chiffon should be used on top.

Threads

Ordinary sewing thread is used for quilting. Thick knitting or tapestry yarn, quilting wool, or colored batting are required for the insertions in shadow Italian or trapunto quilting.

Needles

Appropriately sized embroidery needles are needed to work the quilting. For inserting wool, large-eyed wool needles are required.

Visible filling method

1 Mark the design on the opaque backing fabric and mount it in a frame (pages 100 and 101). Cut out the motif to be applied in felt and baste it lightly in place on the backing, making sure that the knot is underneath and the lines on the backing fabric are covered.

2 Position the transparent top fabric over the work, aligning the grains, then pin and baste it in place. Stitch around the felt motif, with running, back, chain, or any decorative line stitch you like.

Combined shadow work

For shadow Italian quilting, mark the design on the opaque backing fabric and mount the work in a frame (pages 100 and 101). Position the transparent top fabric over the work, aligning the grains, and pin and baste it into place. Work parallel lines of backstitch along the marked lines, as you would for conventional Italian quilting. To work the quilting, loosen the tension of the work in the frame to make the fabrics a little more supple. Thread the colored tapestry or quilting wool in a large-eyed tapestry needle and insert the wool between the lines of stitching as for Italian quilting (page 103).

For shadow trapunto quilting, mark the design and prepare the fabrics as for shadow Italian quilting. Work an outline of backstitch around the motif to be stuffed. Insert colored wool or dyed batting into the back of the work as you would in conventional trapunto quilting (page 102).

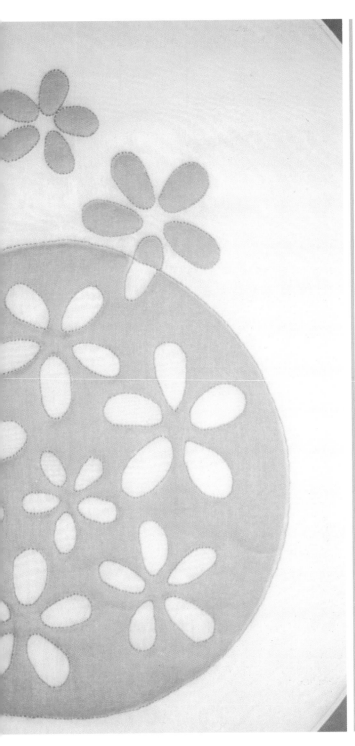

◀ **Mari Yoneyama**
A simple floral motif uses shapes cut from felt.

MACHINE QUILTING

All quilting techniques may be carried out by machine, though the designs may need to be adapted or simplified.

Some sewing machines have accessories such as quilting guides that are specially designed for machine quilting. Also available is a walking foot attachment. This will glide over even very thick layers of batting.

As it is not possible to frame up large pieces of fabric and insert them under the arm of the machine, it is particularly important to baste the layers together carefully. In order to prevent distorting the overall shape of the fabric, always stitch in the same direction from top to bottom, starting from the center of the top edge, then working in the same way toward the sides. For less formal designs, start in the center of the design and work outward.

When finishing an item that has to be a certain size, such as a garment, allow extra fabric, as some shrinkage may take place while quilting.

Fabrics
Most fabrics are amenable to being quilted by machine.

Threads
Sewing thread, buttonhole thread, or quilting thread.

Needles
Sizes 90–100 are best.

Designs
Many designs suitable for hand quilting can also be used for machine work, though intricate patterns and motifs that require continual turning of the work are best avoided. Geometric designs and those with gentle curves, however, are straightforward, and bold or large-scale motifs can easily be stitched by machine.

Quick quilting

Prepare the layers of fabric and batting as for hand quilting, working a grid of basting (page 101). Transfer the design to tracing paper and pin and baste it in position on top of the prepared fabrics.

Set a long stitch length and machine through all layers, following the marked lines on the paper. Start in the center and gradually work outward, smoothing the fabric and tracing as you go. Carefully tear away the paper, take the loose threads to the back of the work, and fasten off.

Using a quilting guide

This useful accessory enables you to stitch parallel lines some distance apart and so it is suitable for diaper (diamond), striped, and grid patterns of straight or wavy lines.

Always work in the same direction from top to bottom or from the same side to avoid puckering the fabric.

Decorative quilting

Italian machine quilting

Although machine quilting is usually worked using a straight machine stitch, zigzag and satin stitch can also be used to great effect when more defined lines are required. Automatic embroidery stitches can also be used to produce more decorative effects, particularly on plain fabrics.

Twin needles spaced either ⅛ or ³⁄₁₆ inch apart are ideal for producing the parallel-line designs needed for this method, using either an opaque top fabric or a transparent one for shadow Italian quilting.

▼ **Machine quilting**
Pauline Brown
A charming decorative effect can be achieved when different stitches are used to machine quilt a solid fabric.

OTHER TECHNIQUES

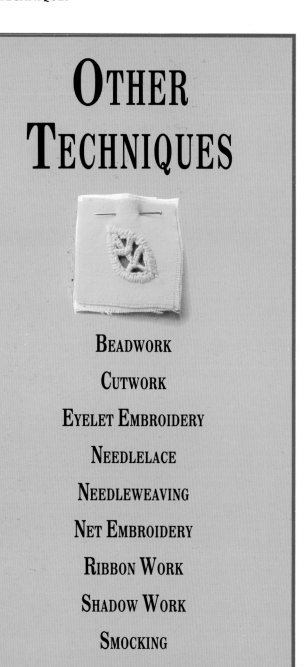

BEADWORK

CUTWORK

EYELET EMBROIDERY

NEEDLELACE

NEEDLEWEAVING

NET EMBROIDERY

RIBBON WORK

SHADOW WORK

SMOCKING

REVERSE SMOCKING

STUMPWORK

Besides the more common embroidery techniques, there are a number of other methods which are interesting to try. They mostly involve the use of familiar stitches, perhaps combined with another type of fabric or a slightly different method of working.

Beadwork, smocking, and ribbon embroidery are mainly used for decorating garments or accessories, but they also are useful for adding texture to an embroidered wallhanging or panel.

In the past, *cutwork and eyelet embroidery* played a big part in the embellishment of table and bed linen. They can still be used for this purpose, but if the openwork aspect of the technique is exploited, new ideas and designs can be developed.

Needlelace and stumpwork are closely related in their use of stitches, but the latter employs a number of special methods and materials to create raised effects.

Needleweaving is a versatile technique which can be worked in association with drawn thread work, on a background fabric, or even across an open space. The weaving may be stitched in regular patterns or freely.

The delicacy of *shadow work and net embroidery* appeals to many embroiderers. Although these techniques are limited in their practical use, the transparent fabrics and pretty stitches are ideal for creating small pictures or garments for special occasions.

BEADWORK

Beads produce an interesting textural surface and are also useful for creating or highlighting small details, while sequins, spangles, shisha glass, and "jewels" add an air of theatricality and glamour.

Fabrics
Beads can be attached to any fabric, though chiffon or voile may need a lightweight backing, such as lawn. Work should be framed for stitching.

Threads
Use a strong thread such as sewing cotton or polyester that is fine enough to pass easily through the hole in the bead or sequin. To further strengthen the thread and prevent it from twisting, pull it through a block of beeswax.

Needles
Beading needles are very long and fine. However, they tend to bend – replace them when this happens.

Designs
Beads catch the light and create textures and patterns that will be a dominant feature of a design.

Stitching individual beads

Textures and patterns can be built up with massed beads and sequins sewn on singly. Sequins may be secured with two or three stitches or held in place by sewing a bead in the center.

Loops and fringes

A number of beads are threaded onto lengths of thread, formed into loops, and the needle inserted close to where it originally emerged. A fringed effect can be made by threading several beads on the thread and then taking the needle back through each one except the one at the bottom end.

Stitching in rows

1 Beads, threaded on a length of thread, are laid on the surface, with a couching thread catching them in place at intervals.

2 Overlapping sequins are each sewn in place with a backstitch, one at a time, in such a way that the stitches are invisible.

Applying shisha glass

1 Hold the mirror glass firmly in place and make two parallel stitches across the glass. Bring the needle out at A, pass it over and back under the first thread, and then repeat this over and under the second thread. Insert the needle at B, then bring it out at C, and repeat the first holding stitch, finishing at D.

2 For the shisha stitch, bring the needle out at E and take it over the intersecting base threads. Make a small stitch alongside the edge of the glass, keeping the thread below the needle. Repeat, taking the thread over the base threads, and working in a clockwise direction around the perimeter of the glass.

CUTWORK

The elaborate cutwork methods of the past are rarely seen today, mainly due to the difficulty and intricacy of the work involved in creating them. However, simple but beautiful cutwork designs can be worked entirely in buttonhole stitch with areas of the background cut away to focus the eye on the main motifs. To progress a stage further to Renaissance cutwork, buttonhole bars are added across the spaces. Stitching picots on the bars is the basis of a lacy effect known as Richelieu cutwork.

Fabrics
A good choice is closely woven linen or medium-weight cotton, which will not fray. It is essential to frame the work to prevent distortion.

Threads
Usually, threads are chosen to match the background fabric or can be slightly darker in tone. Coton à broder, stranded floss, or linen thread are most often used.

Needles
Embroidery needles of a suitable size are best.

Designs
In planning a cutwork design, the relationship between the main motifs and the cutaway background areas needs to be considered. Cutwork requires neat stitching, and the design should be marked on the fabric with an erasable fabric marker. Mark the areas to be cut with an X.

▲ **Pauline Brown**
Hydrangea
Colored cutwork has been worked on a painted background.

Simple cutwork

1 Transfer the design (page 110) precisely but lightly to the fabric, marking the areas that will eventually be cut away with an X. Frame the fabric (page 100) and work small running stitches just inside the outlines and slightly away from the marked areas.

Work close, regular buttonhole stitches (page 20) over the running stitch base, placing the loop of the buttonhole stitch nearest to the area to be cut away.

2 When all the stitching has been completed, carefully cut away the background areas as close as possible to the stitching.

Renaissance cutwork

1 To work buttonhole bars, take the thread across the area to be cut away and make a small stitch to fasten it. Repeat this twice, so that three threads lie together parallel. Work buttonhole stitch over the bar of threads, but not through the fabric. Fasten off and then continue outlining the shape with running stitch.

2 To work branched bars, lay the base threads as for buttonhole bars and work buttonhole stitch halfway along the bar. To form the branch, lay three threads from here across to the edge of the cutwork area and work buttonhole stitch along them back to the first bar. Continue working buttonhole stitch along the rest of the first bar to complete it.

Richelieu cutwork

To work looped picots, lay the base threads as for buttonhole bars (page 27) and work buttonhole stitch halfway along the bar. To form the picot, insert a pin through the fabric at right angles to the bar, loop the thread under the pin, from left to right, over the bar and then under the loop. Twist the working thread around the needle before pulling the thread tightly. Remove the pin and continue working buttonhole stitch along the bar.

EYELET EMBROIDERY

Another cutwork technique, eyelet embroidery or broderie anglaise, came into fashion in the latter half of the 19th century, developing out of a more delicate whitework technique known as Ayrshire embroidery.

Fabrics
Medium-weight cotton or cotton blend fabrics that do not fray are ideal. Frame the fabric as you would for cutwork (page 110).

Threads
These are the same as for other types of cutwork.

Needles
Fine embroidery needles, plus a stiletto for piercing the holes, are required.

Designs
These differ from simple cutwork designs in that it is the holes rather than the spaces between them that are the main feature. Often, floral motifs are made up of eyelet and teardrop shapes. Scalloped edges are the traditional method of finishing.

Eyelet embroidery Preparation

Transfer the design (page 113) and work running stitch around the marked outlines as for cutwork (page 111).

Shaded eyelets
For small shaded eyelets and teardrop shapes (which are overcast with stitches that increase in size to give the original opening an elongated appearance), work a double outline, padding the stitching with lines of running stitch.

Pierced eyelets

For small pierced eyelets, pierce a hole inside the reinforcing running stitches with a stiletto. Work fine overcast stitches over the edge.

Cut eyelets

When making large circular and oval cut eyelets and large teardrop shapes, the fabric must be cut. Clip the fabric from the center of the hole toward the running stitch outline both vertically and horizontally. Turn back the four points to the wrong side and work overcast stitches over the running stitches. Trim away the parts of the points that still protrude from the stitching.

▶ **Kathryn Francis**
Circular and teardrop overcast eyelets are counterbalanced with simple cutwork areas that give strength to this delicate design.

Scalloped edging

The design for a simple semicircular scallop can be made by using a coin to draw the two outlines about ½ inch from the edge of the fabric. Outline both edges with running stitches and pad the area between with more running stitches. Work close buttonhole stitches vertically over the running stitches. When the stitching is complete, trim the excess fabric close to the stitching. Variations in size and design can be used to decorative effect.

NEEDLELACE

Needlelace fillings are networks of delicate stitches that are often incorporated in cutwork (page 111) and drawn thread (page 64) embroidery, when they are usually stitched across the open spaces to give designs more delicacy and interest. They can also be worked as a form of detached embroidery over padding, as in stumpwork (page 124), or stitched free of the background except at the edges, so they are extremely versatile and useful.

Fabrics
Freestanding motifs may be mounted on stiff paper or acetate in order to work them. Needlelace fillings worked on the surface may be stitched on any type of fabric, but should be framed; otherwise, it is very easy to pucker the surrounding fabric.

▶ **Pamela Rooke**
Orchid
A three-dimensional needle-lace piece made on a wired cordonnet incorporates several different stitches.

Threads
Smooth-textured yarns such as crochet cotton, linen thread, coton à broder, or pearl cotton are the most suitable threads. The form of the stitches will be most easily seen when worked in these materials.

Needles
Tapestry needles of suitable size are best as they will not split the threads.

Designs
The technique lends itself to freestyle abstract designs with curved edges. For three-dimensional work, detached buttonhole lace can be manipulated to cover padded areas.

Working on a background

Mark the design on the background (page 10–11), and frame the work (page 100). Outline the shape with small backstitches. This will create a base through which the rows of detached buttonhole fillings are worked. These are attached only by the backstitch outline and do not pass through the fabric, except at the beginning and the end.

Working on a cordonnet

A cordonnet is a continuous double outlining thread that acts as an anchor for freestanding or unsupported needlelace. Fine wire can also be incorporated to make it easier to maintain the outline for the needlelace. Prepare a temporary foundation of supporting layers of fabric, stiff paper, or acetate on which the design has been marked. Couch the cordonnet in place along the outline of the shape to be filled. When the filling stitches have been completed, cut away the couching stitches from the supporting foundation.

Detached buttonhole filling

This is formed in a similar way to surface embroidery buttonhole stitch (page 20), using enough thread to complete the stitching. If working on a backstitch outline, work the first row from left to right, looping the stitch through this and through the backstitch at the end of the row. The second row, worked from right to left, is looped through the first row, and so on. To finish, either loop the last row into the backstitch or background fabric; alternatively, stitch each loop down with a small vertical stitch.

When using a cordonnet loop the detached stitches around the cordonnet. On completion, the ends are darned into the cordonnet.

Straight stitch return

Work the first row of detached buttonhole stitches from left to right, then take the working thread around the outline of backstitches or the cordonnet and return with a straight stitch to the left-hand side.

For the second and subsequent rows, work from left to right, looping the detached buttonhole stitches over the straight stitch return thread as well as the previous row of buttonhole stitches.

This can be worked loosely or to give a firm, solid effect.

1 Work the first buttonhole stitch into the second outlining backstitch, leaving a loose loop. Then work a second buttonhole stitch into the same backstitch, pulling the thread fairly tight. Continue working pairs of buttonhole stitches into alternate backstitches, leaving loops between the pairs.

Double buttonhole filling

2 For the second row, work from right to left, stitching the pairs of buttonhole stitches through the loops of the previous row. A similar but lacier effect can be made with triple groups of buttonhole stitches.

NEEDLEWEAVING

Needleweaving is very often associated with drawn thread work (page 64), but it is also a technique in its own right when worked on the surface or even across an open space or ring. A series of base (warp) threads are laid down alongside one another and then woven together to create either spidery forms or solid areas of pattern. Beads, curtain rings, and metal disks can all be incorporated on the base threads to give an extra interest and texture.

Fabrics
Any firm base fabric is suitable, but it must be stretched in a frame or the fabric will pucker.

Threads
A wide variety of different types of yarn may be used to create different effects.

Needles
Tapestry or large-eyed yarn needles should be used to suit the yarn.

Designs
Needleweaving designs tend to be fairly free-style, often with the base threads radiating from a central point.

Freestyle surface needleweaving

1 Using a fairly thick, strong thread, such as pearl cotton or tapestry or knitting yarn, work a series of long stitches either parallel to one another or radiating from a point. With a contrasting thread, weave under and over groups of the laid stitches, pulling them together or leaving the weaving untensioned to form flat areas of texture.

2 Single laid threads can be wrapped by winding the working thread around them.

Beads and rings

The laid stitches may be threaded through large-holed beads, rings, or washers as the work proceeds. Other beads can be added while weaving. For additional texture, back-stitched needleweaving, as for surface spider's web stitch (page 28), can also be included.

NET EMBROIDERY

Originally developed as a way to imitate lace, this delicate form of embroidery is not often seen today, mainly due to the intricacy involved in creating it. However, it is well worth trying, as the results can be beautiful as well as dainty.

Fabrics
Use hexagonal pattern nylon, cotton, or silk net.

Threads
Fine cotton or silk sewing thread, which usually matches the color of the net is best.

Needles
Use fine tapestry needles.

Designs
The easiest to work are clearly defined designs that include outlined areas suitable for enriching with filling stitches. Geometric patterns and borders can also be incorporated.

◄ **Pamela Rooke**
Rock Pool Box
The main needlewoven elements are raised on small, rolled strips of felt. The hanging pieces are stitched in a similar way to woven picots.

Preparation

With a dark colored felt-tip pen, trace the outline of the design on a sheet of heavy paper. The color of the paper should contrast with that of the net. Baste the net in place over the design.

Stitching
Using a fine cotton or silk thread, work running stitches around the outline, darning in and out of the intersections of the net. To start and finish, darn the ends into the previously worked stitches as inconspicuously as possible.

▶ **Pauline Brown**
Honesty
The seed pods have been depicted by using appliquéd net and organza, with pattern darning.

Stitching filling patterns

All fillings should be worked with as few seams as possible. The most commonly used stitches are running and backstitches, but eyelets and herringbone stitch can also be worked.

The sequence of stitching needs to be worked out before starting; because of its transparency, the underside of the stitching will show through and be part of the finished effect.

RIBBON WORK

There is a variety of ribbons on the market today – single and double-faced satins, velvet, grosgrain, brocade, checked, and printed types.

Their primary use is for trimmings. Apply them by machine, stitching them down either flat, or ruched, gathered or pleated.

In addition, fine ribbons can be used as a type of embroidery thread for stitching on fabric or canvas, creating beautiful textures and decorative effects when used imaginatively.

Threads
For machine or hand appliqué, use ordinary matching sewing thread.

Needles
Large-eyed tapestry or chenille needles are needed when using ribbons for embroidery.

Ribbon on fabric

Choose loosely woven fabric and fine ⅟₁₆- or ⅛-inch-wide ribbon, threaded in a blunt, large-eyed needle. Experiment with surface embroidery stitches, making sure that the ribbon does not twist unintentionally and spoil the stitch. To start and finish, secure the ends of the ribbon with a few stitches in cotton thread.

Ribbon on canvas

The width of the chosen ribbon should match the size of the holes in the canvas.

Most needlepoint stitches (pages 40 to 79) are suitable, but it is important that the ribbon lies flat without twisting.

Stitching ribbon by machine

Wide ribbon can be attached to backing fabric by topstitching along both edges, either with straight or zigzag stitches.

Narrow ribbons are best stitched using an open zigzag stitch, the width being set slightly wider than that of the ribbon.

Ribbons can also be gathered or ruched. To ruche, work a zigzag line of long stitches from edge to edge along the length of the ribbon. Pull up the gathers, then stitch the ruched ribbon in place.

◄ **Caroline Birkett-Harris**
This ribbon embroidery sampler displays a variety of stitches: feather stitch, French knots, herringbone, lazy daisy, fishbone, couching, running stitch, backstitch, and fly stitch, as well as some ribbon weaving.

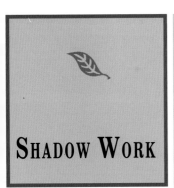

SHADOW WORK

Shadow work was popular in the 18th century when it was one of the fashionable whitework techniques.

Worked on transparent fabric, this method uses mainly close herringbone (or double back) stitch worked on the wrong side of the material, thereby producing a "shadowy" effect when viewed from the right side.

Fabrics
White or very pale transparent fabrics such as organza, organdy, or very fine cotton are most suitable and should be stretched in a frame.

Threads
White or brightly colored stranded floss or silk work best. Always test the depth of color underneath the chosen fabric.

Needles
Fine embroidery needles produce the best results.

Designs
These should be small-scale ones with simple outlines. The design can be traced directly onto the fabric.

Close herringbone stitch

Also known as double backstitch, this is usually worked on the reverse side of the transparent fabric. It is similar to surface embroidery close herringbone (page 21), with each stitch touching. This produces parallel lines of continuous stitches on the right side of the fabric with the "shadow" of the herringbone stitch showing through the fabric between them.

▲ **Kathryn Francis**
Pea Pods
The main leaves and flower are worked in double backstitch; the pea pods are depicted using appliqué and shadow appliqué techniques.

SMOCKING

Best known as the charming traditional decoration on children's dresses, smocking is ideal for controlling and gathering fullness, but can also be used creatively to produce interesting textural effects.

Fabrics
It is usual to choose a fine material that will gather and drape well. When calculating the amount of fabric to buy, allow about three times the width you want the finished piece of smocking to be. It is wise to work a small sample in your chosen fabric before beginning, as different fabrics gather more tightly or loosely than others.

Threads
For gathering, use strong sewing thread in a contrasting color to that of the background fabric. For the smocking, embroidery threads such as stranded floss, coton à broder, and pearl cotton are all suitable. Other yarns can be tried for experimental smocking.

Needles
Any embroidery needle that suits the thread may be used.

Designs
Traditional smocking is usually worked in horizontal bands across the garment. It is essential to count the number of gathers to work out the positioning of the various elements of the design, particularly for those stitches that create zigzags or diamonds.

Preparation
The fabric is gathered into vertical folds by working regular rows of running stitches across the straight grain of the fabric. Unless you own a smocking gathering machine, a grid of dots should be marked on the fabric prior to gathering to keep the stitches, and therefore the folds, uniform.

Marking the dots

1 Iron-on dot transfers are available. Position and pin the transfer face down on the wrong side of the fabric, so that the dots follow the grain. Press with a medium-hot iron.

2 Alternatively, to make your own grid, place a piece of graph paper on the wrong side of the fabric with a sheet of dressmakers' carbon paper between. Mark a dot with a ballpoint pen at the appropriate measured intersection.

Gathering

Thread the needle with a length of sewing thread slightly longer than the width of the fabric. Knot the end and work even running stitches, picking up a tiny amount of fabric at each dot. Leave the thread hanging and start a new one for each row.

Pulling up and fastening off

When all the rows have been completed, pull up the threads in pairs to the required width so that the folds lie evenly. Tie the pairs of threads together to hold the folds in place.

Stitching
Smocking is usually worked from left to right across the folds in the chosen pattern, with each stitch involving picking up a small amount of fabric at the centerline of the fold. To begin, the thread is brought through the first left-hand fold slightly to the left of the centerline, and to finish, it is taken down to the right of the centerline of, and through, the last fold, fastening off with a double backstitch on the wrong side.

Stem and mock chain

Stem (or outline) stitch is a tightly tensioned stitch, made in a similar way to surface embroidery stem stitch (page 16). Bring the needle up at A, take the thread over two folds, keeping it above the needle, then insert it at B and bring it out at C to repeat.

This can be reversed, and if two rows are worked close together, reversing the second, it produces mock chain stitch.

Cable stitch

Make the first stitch over two folds as for stem stitch, keeping the thread above the needle. Make the next stitch with the thread below the needle over folds 2 and 3. Continue across the work, making stitches over two folds with the thread alternately above and below the needle. Double cable stitch consists of two rows of cable stitch in which the second row forms a mirror image of the first.

Wave and trellis stitches

These are worked in zigzag formation in steps across the work. The stitches are similar to stem stitch, with the needle being slightly angled as it emerges above or below the thread. For the downward steps, the thread is kept above the needle; for the upward steps it remains below. Trellis stitch is formed by working two or more rows of wave stitch in opposite directions to create a diamond pattern.

Diamond stitch

Work a stem stitch over two folds, keeping the thread above the needle and bringing the needle out between the folds. Take the thread down diagonally and insert the needle between folds 3 and 4. Work a stem stitch over folds 3 and 4 with the thread below the needle before taking it diagonally up to folds 5 and 6. Repeat.

Surface honeycomb stitch

This is worked in a similar way to diamond stitch, but make the first stitch over folds 1 and 2 and the second over folds 2 and 3.

◄ **Fiona Lewis**
Diamond, feather, surface honeycomb, honeycomb, double cable, trellis, and stem stitches are all used on this sampler.

Honeycomb stitch

This double stitch groups the folds of fabric together in pairs to form a delicate cell-like appearance. Bring the needle out at A, insert it at B, picking up folds 2 and 1, then bring it out again at C, just below A. Repeat the stitch to D, but this time angle it down through the fold to the left-hand side of fold 2. Take the next set of double stitches over folds 2 and 3. Repeat, alternating the position of the double stitches to the end of the row.

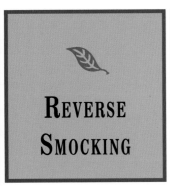

REVERSE SMOCKING

Reverse smocking differs from traditional smocking in that the stitches are worked on the back to form a textured surface.

A development of this technique is Canadian or North American smocking. It differs from the usual method of working in that the preparatory gathering is omitted, and the fabric is ruched or pleated either from the front or the back of the work, depending on the design.

Fabrics
Reverse smocking is often used for pillow covers made from velvet or satin, but can be worked experimentally for textured articles and wallhangings in many different fabrics.

Threads
Strong thread, such as linen or button thread, that matches the fabric is used for picking up the marked dots and stitching them together to form the patterns.

Reverse smocking

For reverse smocking, the gathered fabric is stitched from the back, using rows of stem stitch to preserve the folds so that no stitching is visible on the front.

Lattice pattern

Mark out the grid on the wrong side of the fabric with a water-soluble pen. Using strong thread, knotted at one end, pick up a small amount of fabric at A; then pick up dot B, then dot A again, pulling A and B tightly together with a small stitch. Move down to C, keeping the thread slack between A/B and C. Pick up the dots at C and D, bringing them together before moving on to E. Continue down the length of the grid. Then work the second row, repeating across the width of the grid.

Flower pattern

Mark the grid on the right side of the fabric. Pick up a small amount of fabric at A with a diagonal stitch, proceed to B, C and D and back to A. Pull the thread tightly, drawing the four corners of the square together and secure with a backstitch. Take the thread to the back of the work, ready to stitch the second square. Keep the fabric flat between each square.

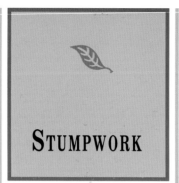

STUMPWORK

Raised embroidery was always an integral part of the repertoire used in the ecclesiastical embroideries of the Middle Ages, but became more prominent in the 1600s when it was often stitched by young girls to form elaborate decoration for pictures, boxes, and mirror frames.

Three-dimensional effects are very much a part of textile work today, and the techniques of stumpwork are still used since they are an ideal way of producing interesting results.

Fabrics
Any firm, closely woven background fabric can be used. It must be stretched in a frame to prevent distortion.

Threads
A variety of smooth-textured yarns, including stranded floss, coton à broder, and pearl cotton are all suitable.

Needles
Embroidery needles are usual, with tapestry needles ideal for the detached stitches.

Designs
Although the designs of the past generally consisted of a series of motifs arranged in a haphazard fashion, today's embroiderers usually seek more integrated effects. Natural forms, such as fruit and flowers, figures and architectural features, have all provided design ideas. The scale of stumpwork is usually fairly small, so the technique requires dexterity and good workmanship.

Stitches
The majority of stitches used to produce the raised effects of stumpwork are also found in other types of embroidery where their effect is likely to be less textured.

Particular stitches for stumpwork
Bullion knots (page 30). Detached buttonhole stitch (page 115). French knots (page 30). Padded satin stitch (page 24). Raised cup stitch (page 29). Tent stitch slips (page 40). Woven picots (page 27).

▲ **Barbara Hirst**
The Chiltern Farmer
The sheep is worked as a slip in pendant couching (page 17), with a padded leather head. Needlelace (page 114) worked on a wire cordonnet creates the farmer's garments.

Slips

These are small motifs that are embroidered separately from the main design, then cut out and stitched in place. Needlepoint slips are usually worked in silk or wool in tent stitch on fine canvas.

Small fabric slips are first embroidered with stitches such as French or bullion knots covering the surface. These are then usually padded and applied to the surface.

Padded appliqué

This type of padded shape differs from fabric slips in that the embroidery is done *after* the motif has been stitched in place. Work in a similar way to padded appliqué with turned-under edges (page 94), adding stitches to decorate.

Using craft interfacing

Cut out the motif in heavy craft interfacing and baste it lightly to the background fabric. Work satin stitch evenly to cover the interfacing. To do this, it may be helpful to begin at the middle of the motif, work outward one way, and then work from the center out the other way to complete.

Freestanding wire shapes

Cut a length of fine florists' wire long enough to encircle the shape and wrap it with stranded floss. Start by tying the floss to the wire and bending the end of the wire over it to hold it on. Wrap tightly and smoothly, finishing in the same way you started. Twist the ends of the wire together and bend to form the required shape. This can then be filled with needlelace (page 115).

Modeling clay bases

Wooden molds (the original "stumps" that gave stumpwork its name) were used as a basis for heads, figures, fruits, and so on. A modern replacement is self-hardening modeling clay, which can be selected for its color or completely covered with stitches or fabric. Before the clay hardens, make two or three small holes at the edges of the mold through which a securing stitch can be made to attach it to the background fabric.

Wrapping vellum

Although vellum was originally used for this technique, thin cardboard or heavy craft interfacing make suitable substitutes.

Cut a narrow strip of vellum of the required length. Lay the end of a length of stranded floss along the vellum, toward one end. Start wrapping the vellum evenly and smoothly until the whole length is covered. Thread the end of the floss into a tapestry needle and bring it back through the wrapping to complete.

The wrapped lengths can be couched down in a variety of loops, twists, or folds which stand away from the surface.

▲ Barbara Hirst
Henry VIII
The head of this fine portrait has been soft-sculpted from muslin. The sumptuous clothing is created with needlelace, tiny Victorian beads, semiprecious stones and pearls, and bits of ostrich feather.

The embroideries of this talented stumpwork artist are always worked in threads no thicker than 100/3 silk.

Raised leaf stitch

Cut a narrow strip of cardboard about ¼ × 2 inches to use as a template. Bring a needle threaded with pearl cotton up at A, alongside the cardboard. Work six to eight satin stitches over the cardboard, keeping it in an upright position on the surface of the fabric.

Bring the needle up at B and thread it through the stitches to the beginning. Remove the cardboard carefully and pull the loops back; inserting the needle at C to produce a slightly raised leaf shape.

Banksia rose stitch

To form the center of the rose, bring the needle out at A and take it down close by, leaving a small loop. Work several loops the same size close together and secure the last one with a backstitch. Then, work four loose stem stitches (page 16) encircling the loops. Continue working stem stitch, gradually decreasing the tension and increasing the number so that by the fourth row the rose is complete.

▼ **Barbara Hirst**
Samurai Three
This dramatic figure is clad in needlelace embellished with gold leather and gold machine threads and with fine beading wire worked as an integral part of the cordonnet. The head has been soft-sculpted from muslin.

THEMES

Embroidery can be used to interpret different subjects in a variety of decorative styles, but the wide choice of techniques, fabrics, and threads also offers plenty of scope for developing an innovative personal style. Very often, a new technique or an exciting fabric will spark off an idea for a project. Embroidery is so versatile that it can be used creatively for pictures and panels, for items for the home, for garments and accessories, and also for three-dimensional objects. Studying the work of other embroiderers will enable you to see how other artists have interpreted a subject and help give you the confidence to experiment.

LANDSCAPE

Painters have always been inspired by the landscape, whether it is a classic country view, a beautiful sunset, or a dynamic seascape. For embroiderers, this source of subject matter has a similar appeal, with the added attraction that a wide range of techniques can be utilized in many different materials and threads, to create texture, depth, and so on.

Designs for landscape, townscape, architecture, or interiors can be sketched and notes made as to the colors, textures, mood, and atmosphere of the scene. This will help you to

determine the qualities you want to put across in the embroidery and give you ideas for the method, fabrics, and thread to use. Alternatively, you can take your inspiration from photographs or other visual reference material. These can be modified and adapted to suit your preferences, the scale can be adjusted, colors changed and certain aspects of the design accentuated or played down as you like.

The techniques used most often to create realistic depictions of landscapes are surface and machine stitches, together with fabric paints and appliqué.

Fabrics can be chosen to coincide with the textural qualities of the scene – for example, a heavily ribbed brown woolen material or corduroy can be used to depict furrows in a plowed field, while a ruched silky fabric could simulate the ripples of the sea.

Threads, too, may be chosen for their color and texture, and the direction in which the stitches are worked will have a bearing on the mood and realism of the piece.

For a somewhat more stylized effect, needlepoint and counted cross stitch are very popular. If the other counted thread methods are used, the result is usually more abstract.

◀ Pauline Brown
Herbaceous Border
7 × 10 inches

This piece demonstrates the successful combination of a free approach with conventional needlepoint stitches. Surface embroidery stitches, ribbons, and appliqué are added for textural effect. The foxgloves are made from tiny rolled-up pieces of fabric, and the foreground area includes three-dimensional leaves worked in Milanese stitch.

▼ Lydia Solomon
Cornfield
19 × 23 inches

Fabric paints were used to create the sky and background before the fields and fence posts were machine-stitched. The foreground area is more densely stitched by hand, mainly using straight stitches, couching, and bullion and French knots.

◀ Lydia Solomon
Home Thoughts from Abroad
18½ × 22 inches

This realistic effect has been achieved by working over a fabric-painted background with machine-stitched whip and satin stitches. The blossoms and foreground are mainly depicted with hand-worked French knots and straight stitch.

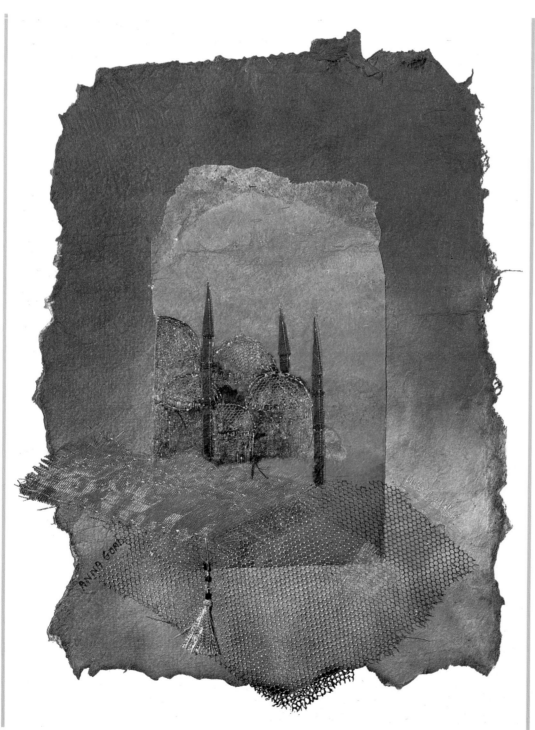

◄ Anna Goad
Images of the Orient II
11½ × 8 inches

This is one of a number of pieces inspired by the exotic atmosphere of vacations in Morocco and Turkey. Transparent fabrics, nets, and silks are bonded and hand-stitched to a background of dyed silks, and handmade and dyed paper.

► Anna Goad
Images of the Orient III
11½ × 8 inches

A visit to the Blue Mosque in Istanbul provided the inspiration for this piece, which superimposes stitched transparent fabrics on a background of handmade paper.

► Wendy Lees
The Fountain
20 × 14 inches

The artist's aim when creating this layered fabric piece was to capture in stitches the fine spray and the mystical light against the background of dark trees. Beads, sequins, and hand embroidery have their own special part to play in creating the right effect.

▲ **Elizabeth de Clermont**
Morris Hall with Peanut Playing
12 × 12 inches

The inner picture of the embroiderer's home is worked in appliqué, and the details are picked out in surface stitches. This is framed with a needle-point border, mainly worked in wool yarn, with the trees wrapped in gold and wool thread.

▼ Margaret Pascoe
Towers and Flowers
39 × 22½ inches

The starting point for this blackwork embroidery was a newspaper clipping of a skyscraper in London. The unusual way in which the technique is worked incorporates black threads of many thicknesses, plus colored stranded floss. The directions in which the stitches are worked give form to the shape of the building.

▶ Ann Danielson
Burning Stubble
13 × 16 inches

This embroidery was inspired by fields of burning stubble seen in the evening light. Strips of layered and frayed fabrics are sewn on a cotton base fabric. The Cretan stitch worked in a haphazard fashion successfully evokes the impression of the wheat in the foreground.

▼ **Ann Wheeler**
Indian Palace
29½ × 20 inches

This abstract hanging depicting a landscape is one of a series of pieces inspired by the architecture of India. Its muted, hand-dyed colors and machine embroidery with metallic threads evoke an air of mystery.

◀ **Margaret Pascoe**
Three Trees
16½ × 15 inches

Straight stitches worked in different directions—vertical, horizontal, and diagonal—over counted threads produce variations in density and tonal value and break up the formality of the design.

▲ **Alison King**
Hillside, Amulree
36 × 30 inches

The emotional atmosphere of this landscape has been captured by using a variety of different fabrics, including hand-dyed felts, and paper; some extend onto the mount. Machine embroidery provides texture and detail.

▲ **Anna Christy**
Cretan Woman with Flowers
5½ × 4 inches

Inspired by the artist's drawn and photographic reference, this realistic embroidery was achieved by using the stitches and threads as if they were a drawing medium. These stitches are densely worked to cover the background fabric, and the directions in which the stitches are worked help to create the different textures that make up the scene.

▶ **Margaret Burdett**
Cyprus Valley (detail)
23½ × 25 inches

The colors and textural qualities of the bark of the eucalyptus trees are depicted by means of needlepoint in wool yarn and silk on a background of dyed and transparent fabrics. The foreground area is worked in quilting, using wrapped canes and strips of balsa wood.

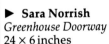

◄ Jean Bow
Summer Garden
20 × 17 inches

Brown burlap sponged with dye provides an alternative to the fabrics conventionally used for pulled work. The garden scene is created by means of a range of eyelets, combined with satin stitch and a variety of other stitches. The work has been mounted on a strongly colored blue lining which shows through the embroidery and gives an additional lift to the work.

► Sara Norrish
Greenhouse Doorway
24 × 6 inches

Having completed a series of paintings of greenhouses, gardens, and solariums, the artist experimented with the theme in embroidery, resulting in this piece. Layers of fabrics, including chiffon, net, and scrim, were machine embroidered with various stitches, including free machine work, and cable and whip stitches, creating a lush, textured foreground.

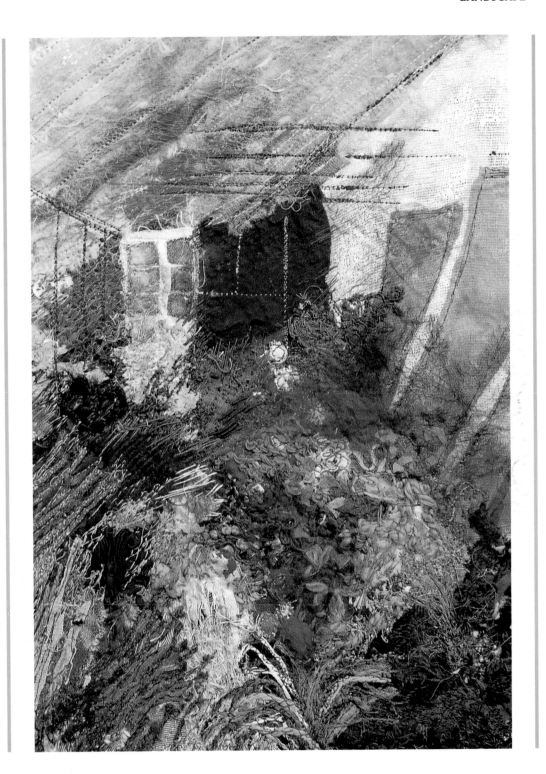

PEOPLE AND ANIMALS

Depicting the human figure in embroidery can be a rather daunting prospect unless you are experienced in drawing from life. This is an obvious starting point and a sound foundation on which to base designs that are to have a degree of realism about them. For inexperienced artists, however, a simpler alternative is to use family photographs, vacation snapshots, or magazine clippings, all of which can provide suitable reference material for developing successful designs.

The human form may be static or captured in movement. The right treatment will depend on the degree of detail required – whether it is depicted in close-up, at a distance, or simply in silhouette.

Faces and heads, including masks, make interesting subjects, especially when they are carried out in a decorative or stylized manner.

Producing caricatures can be a delightful way of overcoming the difficulty of depicting the face or figure realistically, and this treatment can also

be used for designs based on animals.

The animal world offers a wealth of interesting subject matter, from pets to wild animals. Also included in this category are butterflies, insects, birds, and fish, many of which have interesting patterns and textures that are easy to depict in embroidery.

Sketching animals is likely to be difficult as they generally do not stay still for very long, but designs can be developed from photographs or reference books on natural history.

There is no restriction on the techniques suitable for developing designs based on people and animals. Some of the raised and padded techniques, such as appliqué, quilting, and stumpwork, offer the chance to create designs in high- or low-relief, giving form to the subject.

Designs which include some of the more decorative birds, fish, or insects can be worked using intricate surface stitchery, needlepoint, metal thread work, or counted thread techniques.

◀ Wendy Lees
Boy with Two Ice-creams
18½ × 14 inches

Recreated from photographic reference material, the effect of the running boy has been developed by using a series of straight stitches on a foundation of applied chiffons and nets. The silhouetted figure in the background counterbalances that of the main subject.

◀ Janet Haigh
The Whitaker Family
36 × 20 inches

This commissioned sampler contains imagery of people, animals, and places important to the owner. Many different types of embroidery have been used, making it a sampler for the artist as well as the client. These include appliqué, needlepoint, beadwork, crewel work, and counted thread embroidery in a wide variety of fabrics and threads.

▶ Wendy Lees
Boy Seated
55 × 43 inches

Taken from a pastel drawing of a model at a life class, this machine-quilted wallhanging has been created from solid-colored cotton fabrics. They have been further strengthened by the outlines of the black background which shows between the appliquéd fabrics.

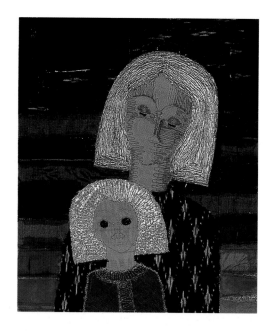

▲ **Rose Verney**
Radha and Krishna
72 × 72 inches

Part of a set which was commissioned to hang over a bed, this hand-pieced appliqué relies for its effect on the strength of the figures and surrounding decor contrasted with the black background. Details have been embroidered by hand, with beads and jewels added.

▶ **Liz Harding**
Crocodile
23½ × 36 inches

This charming embroidery was based on a postcard of Ethiopian children. Layers of soft cotton and felt have been stitched together with running stitches. Colored cotton and silk fabrics have been appliquéd with hand and machine stitching.

◄ Gisela Banbury
Mother and Child
25½ × 18 inches

The arrival of a baby in the family prompted this stylized version of a well-loved subject. An appliquéd background in strips of different fabrics serves as a foil for the figures, which are also appliquéd. The faces are treated in a simple but effective way with a minimum of hand and machine stitching.

► Karen Howse
Procession
24 × 10 inches

A trip to northern India influenced this mixed-media work, which brings together fragments of machine embroidery linked with pieces of wire and cane. The aim in creating this embroidery is to conjure up a textile "icon" which is rich in color and textural variety.

▼ Janet Haigh
Clarice Cliff
18 × 12 inches

The designs of a well-known decorator of pottery inspired this appliqué picture. The figure stands in a "landscape" of typical motifs taken from her china. Parts of this decorative background have been hand-painted and enhanced with surface stitches.

▲ **Karen Howse**
Three Monks (detail)

A mixed media piece in the
same series as "Procession"
(page 141). The three robed
figures are set in a mystical
landscape.

◀ **Sonda Galsworthy**
Statue of Liberty
12 × 8 inches

This interpretation in blackwork uses a variety of conventional stitches, and the emphasis on the tonal values in the design gives form to the figure. Outlines are used only in some areas to strengthen the shapes.

◀ **Yvonne Morton**
Celestial Serpent
9½ × 6 inches

The winged serpent presides over the heavens – the sun, moon, and stars – in this decorative piece, which combines richly painted fabrics for the appliqué and quilting with free machine work.

▲ **Belinda Montagu**
Domus
12 × 10 feet

The first of four wallhangings commissioned by Lord Montagu which depict the history of Beaulieu Abbey, this is a multimedia piece. It was made in sections and then assembled. The faces and many of the birds and animals were worked in needlepoint, while other techniques used include patchwork, appliqué, quilting, machine embroidery and couched gold threads.

▼ **Ailsa M. Findlay**
Frieze from a Temple in Angkor Wat, Cambodia
27 × 48 inches

Based on a rubbing of a Cambodian temple frieze, this example of hand appliqué on linen employs a wide variety of fabrics, plus other components, such as feathers, lace, cord, leather, wood, and string.

▶ **Morag Gilbert**
Silly Cow
12 × 12 inches

This commissioned piece is a play on words. The image was drawn by free machine stitching on the wool background. Details were then added by hand in cotton and silk threads to give color and form to the piece.

▼ Niamh McCarthy
Brent Geese
11½ × 8 inches

The annual arrival of the geese from Greenland for their winter sojourn in Dublin sparked off the idea for this needlepoint piece. The interesting use of Bargello stitch, worked on the diagonal, produces the wonderful winter sky. Leaf stitch creates the effect of feathers, while Jacquard, Milanese, and fan stitch are used for the other parts of the birds.

▶ Elspeth Kemp
Dove Ascending (detail of altar frontal)

Metal thread embroidery is often used for ecclesiastical embroidery because of its richly decorative effect. Here it is combined with appliqué and couching in a symmetrical design. The body of the bird is worked in basket stitch over a foundation of string; the rest of the raised areas are padded with felt.

▲ Belinda Montagu
Firescreen
30 × 24 inches

A combination of techniques was used to make this embroidered firescreen. The ducks were first stitched on canvas and then appliquéd to the background, which had been prepared with machine appliqué and surface embroidery.

FLOWERS AND PLANTS

This subject area has long been a favorite with embroiderers. The Elizabethans, Stuarts, and Georgians decorated their garments with detailed floral motifs, and the Victorians embroidered posies, wreaths, and sprays of flowers on all manner of household items as well as clothing.

Collecting reference material is particularly simple. Whether you live in a town, a city, or the country, parks, gardens, and florists are all close at hand for personal study, and a visit to the library will provide books with botanical illustrations. Gardening magazines and seed catalogs are easily obtainable and often have good close-up photographs.

Flowers can be embroidered in a realistic fashion with attention to detail, shading, and form, or you may prefer to treat them in an impressionistic or stylized way, while still capturing the essence and unique characteristic of

each particular species.

For a middle-distance view of a group of plants, look particularly at the movement, rhythm, and direction of growth, as well as the overall shape and textural quality.

Surface embroidery is probably the most popular method for depicting flowers realistically, but this is by no means the only way in which such effects can be achieved. The smooth texture of freestyle machine embroidery will create equally convincing realism and the use of multicolored and *ombré* threads can produce the necessary subtle shading. Three-dimensional effects can be achieved by using wired needlelace and stumpwork techniques, or individual flowers can be fashioned from pieces of fabric cut to shape. Needlepoint, crewel work, and laid work are ideal for creating stylized designs, and cutwork and other whitework techniques are often used for floral subjects.

Gila Mader
Summer Garden (detail)

The rich texture combined with strong color are the main features of this wool embroidery. Stitches used include knots, couching, and straight stitches, with rolls and strips of felt attached by hand.

▶ **Greta Fitchett**
Suburban Jungle
40 × 26 inches

The richly colored background for this wallhanging was hand-dyed and machine embroidered. The free-standing flowers and leaves were created by machine stitching on dissolvable fabric and then applying them to the background.

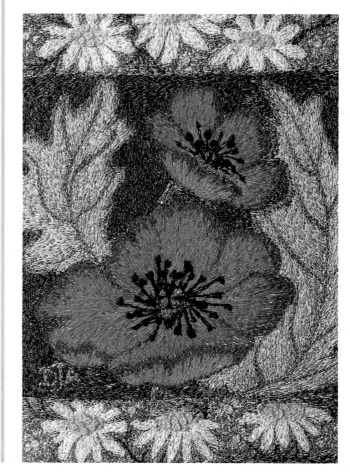

▲ **Greta Fitchett**
Delphiniums
36 × 26 inches

The velvet background throws the lighter colors of the appliquéd satins and sheers into sharp contrast. Texture is provided by means of buttons and surface and machine stitchery, together with Suffolk puffs (small motifs made from gathered circles of fabric).

◄ **Sarah W. Mitchell**
Reflections
24 × 26 inches

The interesting composition of this piece relies for its effect on the differing scale of the four jigsaw areas. A variety of fabrics and threads have been incorporated, with a combination of hand and machine stitches being used. The poppies in the foreground are made from manipulated silk with hand stitching, while the large bloom is made from painted silk.

◄ **Daphne J. Ashby**
Poppies and Daisies
7 × 5 inches

Solidly worked free machine embroidery on cotton, using a variety of threads, creates a realistic effect. French knots worked in the centers of the flowers complete the picture.

► **Daphne J. Ashby**
Hellebore Niger
17 × 14 inches

This successful combination of techniques includes a needlepoint background, a variety of other stitches, and French knots, plus appliquéd flowers and leaves made from silk with beads and stitches added to complete the effect.

This is one of a series of sunflower pictures worked after a visit to France. Mono-printed fabric was cut up and appliquéd to a painted background, and machine embroidery was then densely worked over it.

▶ **Sandra Grant**
Lilies
27½ × 10 inches

A free-form representation of orange lilies, the piece was created in a similar way to "Yellow Tulips" (right).

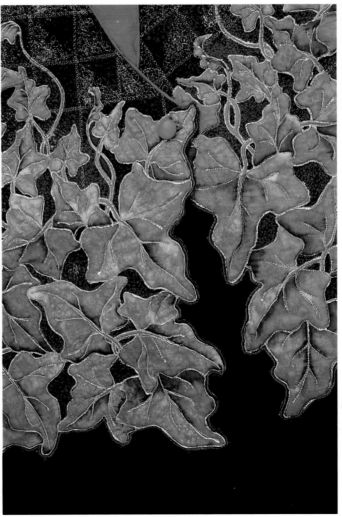

▼ Anita Faithfull
Painted Waistcoat

Using her garden as a source of inspiration, the artist has captured the many shades of the leaves by using silk paints on habutai silk, which she has then quilted by machine using a shiny thread. The vibrancy of the leaves contrasts with the painted and machine-stitched geometric design of the background.

▲ Sandra Grant
Yellow Tulips
16 × 20 inches

This stunning depiction of realistic three-dimensional tulips is stitched to a background made from layers of fine fabrics stitched together by machine with colored threads, the stitching creating a painterly effect. The tulips and leaves were wired to give them their shape and then attached to wired and wrapped stalks.

▲ **Maggie Phillips**
Water Garden
14 × 14 inches

Painted linen forms the basis
of the watery background here
with appliquéd nets and
tarlatan. Machine embroidery
creates the vegetation. The
needlepoint mount is worked
with Rhodes, tent, and straight
Gobelin stitches.

▶ **Pamela Rooke**
Clematis Montana
8 × 8 inches

The geometric pattern of the
transfer-painted background,
which represents an open-
work screening wall, acts as a
contrast to the natural forms of
the clematis. The flower
shapes are worked in layers of
fabric with gold metal thread
embroidery.

◀ Margaret Griffiths
Jardinière
18 × 18 inches

For this well-loved subject, a number of hand and machine-stitched techniques have been incorporated on a painted background. The vase has been trapunto-quilted, and the butterflies have been worked in machine-made lace. Stitches include French knots, woven wheels, and needleweaving in a variety of different threads.

▼ Peggy Field
The Yellow Carpet
30 × 30 inches

The interesting background of this piece was achieved by spray-dyeing around hand-made templates onto four layers of organdy, which were then machine-embroidered. The vase is appliquéd, and the flowers are worked mainly in long, straight hand stitches.

ABSTRACTS

Abstract designs can be developed from almost any source. Realistic images can be adapted, reduced, or embellished so that the result only vaguely resembles the original form. Abstract patterns can also be based on geometric shapes, lines, or random motifs. Embroidery designs can arise from doodles and "accidental" designs, such as ink blots or reflections in puddles or shadows. These may be rhythmic and flowing, rigid, or spiky, with colors that can be changed to reflect your personality – indeed emotions, moods, and abstract feelings can all be linked to particular colors, textures, and shapes. Many embroiderers gain inspiration from the embroidery materials themselves, producing work which relies mainly on color or texture for its effect.

Some of the counted thread techniques, such as Hardanger and drawn thread work, rely for their impact on the strong abstract geometric forms which are inherent in their construction. Pulled work, blackwork, and counted cross stitch can also be used for abstract designs.

The freedom of machine embroidery is particularly suited to abstraction – drawing in a random fashion with the needle can produce an interesting starting point which can be developed further as the work progresses.

Appliquéd and quilted fabrics, haphazardly arranged, make a good basis on which to stitch freely, resulting in highly textured and colorful pieces.

▼ Corliss Miller
Elizabethan Frame
9 × 10 inches

Potato and sponge prints in gold and pearlized acrylic paints have been appliquéd to this highly decorative quilted and machine-embroidered piece. The design was based on a study of the costume and embroidery of the Elizabethan period in England.

◄ Avril Lansdell
Treasure Hoard
8½ × 7 inches

This small piece displays a formal approach to spider's web stitch. It is based on a chain stitch grid, containing stitches and pieces of appliquéd fabrics.

▲ Karen Howse
Midsummer Shade
8 × 13 inches

In this constructed piece, which uses images of India as a starting point, a series of machine-embroidered elements have been assembled. Cane, wire and beads are successfully used in combination with fabric and thread.

◄ Cynthia Pearson
Flower Patch II
18 × 18 inches

Using a background of cotton velvet, the center of the piece was built up by means of layers of machine stitching. The aim is to convey an impression of the green lawned areas often found in suburban gardens in conjuction with the rich strong colors of summer flowers.

► Helen Collinson
Quilted Butterfly Garden
18 × 18 inches

This immaculate work, based on a Japanese temple garden, combines a variety of techniques, including machine and hand quilting, shadow quilting, and appliqué. The design has been carefully conceived to include a number of different patterns.

► Avril Lansdell
Seashore
9 × 12 inches

This panel shows the use of spider's web stitch in a semi-abstract work. A patchwork of thin fabrics was diagonally quilted, and the variety of stitches used gives the impression of a sandy beach with wooden pilings and a rock pool.

▲ Helen Collinson
Quilted Butterfly Garden (detail)

A close-up view of this Japanese-influenced embroidery clearly shows the techniques used, including the appliquéd butterflies and couched cords.

◄ Helen Collinson
Salmon and Gold Square (detail)

Balance and proportion are key elements in the design of this piece, which includes Japanese papers, fabric-covered card and wrapping techniques. The harmonizing colors are offset by the lustre of the gold threads, which create texture and interest.

◀ Vanessa Blackmoor
Her Passage Through the Trees
17½ × 19 inches

Thinking about an "Alice in Wonderland" theme led to the idea of creating an image that would represent Alice's transition between the ordinary and dream worlds. The central hand-stitched panel is surrounded by a patchwork of different fabrics.

▼ Judy Hope
Rocks and Crystals
6 × 4 inches

Photographs of underground caves prompted a series of embroideries in different techniques. For this example, hand-dyed felt circles were applied with herringbone and Cretan stitch to the painted and textured background.

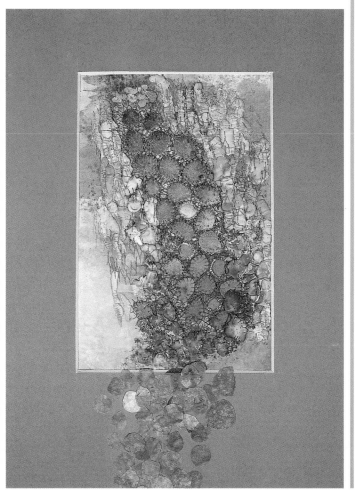

▲ Helen Pincus
Mordent
13 × 10 inches

Based on musical forms, selected widths of cardboard and rods have been hand-wrapped with knitting ribbon and then couched in place on an aluminum mesh base.

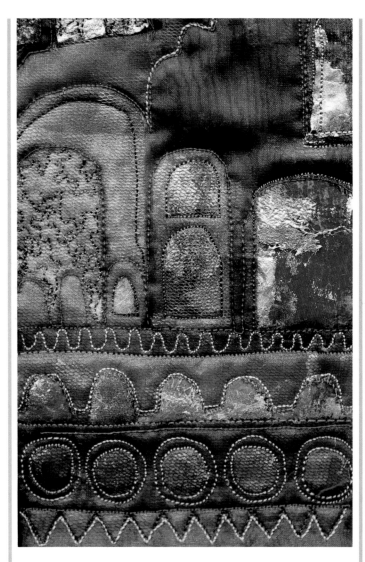

◄ **Yvonne Morton**
Byzantine II (detail)

A study of Byzantine architecture prompted a series of embroideries in richly quilted fabrics, layers of which were built up, painted, and stitched to achieve this sumptuous effect.

► **Gisela Banbury**
5 × 7 inches

A variation on the "spark plug" theme (right), this repeat needlepoint piece in stranded floss and pearl cotton contains a variety of stitches including tent, cross, upright cross, Smyrna and Gobelin.

► **Charlotte Hodge**
Sundance
17 × 32 inches

The impact of the vibrant colors is an integral part of this hand-stitched appliquéd piece. The frayed edges of the pieces of silk and the transparency of others add detail to the bold effect.

◄ **Gisela Banbury**
9½ × 6 inches

Repeat geometric designs may be evolved from many different sources. The original inspiration for this Hardanger embroidery was a drawing of the top of a spark plug.

OBJECTS AND GARMENTS

One of the great advantages of embroidery is that it is so versatile. Not only can the various techniques be used for creating pictures, panels, and decorative wallhangings, but they can be adapted for use on garments and accessories, as well as being used to decorate three-dimensional objects.

To use embroidery on garments was, in the past, the prerogative of the rich, but, today, quilted and machine-embroidered garments have become readily available. Embroiderers, though, are able to create out-of-the-ordinary designs for use on clothes simply to add individuality.

Accessories such as bags and belts readily lend themselves to being embellished with embroidery, and small items such as brooches, pendants, and buckles can also be stitched. An innovation in embroidery is to make and decorate three-dimensional, constructed pieces. These can be totally abstract or can realistically simulate natural or manmade forms.

When using embroidery for garments, thought

needs to be given to the use to which the article will be put. Machine appliqué and quilting are hardwearing and therefore suitable for everyday clothing and children's wear, but beading and fine, delicate work would be more appropriate for infrequently worn items, such as an evening dress.

Bags of all types can be embroidered, and the same consideration as to use applies. Needlepoint would be hardwearing for a handbag or shopping bag, while evening bags embellished with beads and surface stitches can be embroidered to complement evening wear.

Small three-dimensional pieces of jewelry, made by using machine embroidery or lace, can be fashioned for a delicate effect; more substantial pieces can be embroidered and stiffened to make them more robust.

For three-dimensional articles, foundations of cardboard or wood can be covered with previously embroidered fabrics; padded appliqué shapes can be wired so that they become free-standing, and machine lace using dissolvable fabrics can be stiffened to hold its shape.

◄ Judy Clayton
Embroidered Bowl
10 × 7 inches

The bubbly texture is achieved by using transparent plastic, silks, sequin waste, and metallic threads machine embroidered with whip stitch on a base of fabric dissolvable in hot water. This is shrunk and molded to form the shape.

▼ Juliet Walker
Hand-held Fan
18 inches in diameter

The colors and textures of this piece were inspired by marine life. Handmade paper has been combined with machine embroidery and a machine-lace edging. Beads and sequins give additional sparkle and texture.

◄ Karen Holt
Brooch 2
5 × 3½ inches

Scraps of fabrics are densely machine embroidered on a muslin base with the outlines in braid. The embroidery is backed with heavy interfacing so that it holds its shape and then varnished to make it rigid.

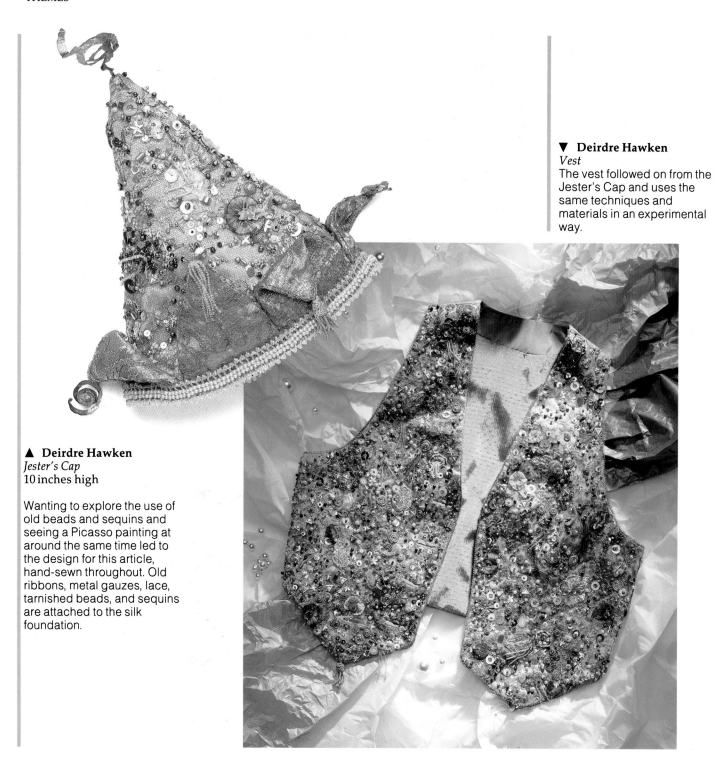

▼ **Deirdre Hawken**
Vest
The vest followed on from the Jester's Cap and uses the same techniques and materials in an experimental way.

▲ **Deirdre Hawken**
Jester's Cap
10 inches high

Wanting to explore the use of old beads and sequins and seeing a Picasso painting at around the same time led to the design for this article, hand-sewn throughout. Old ribbons, metal gauzes, lace, tarnished beads, and sequins are attached to the silk foundation.

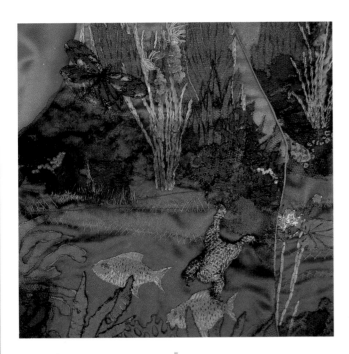

Janet Morris
Pisces vest (detail)

Layered fine fabrics are combined with surface stitchery, including needleweaving and some beading. The motifs are made from crystal organza bonded to satin.

▶ **Karen Holt**
Brooch 1
5 × 2 inches

Scraps of fabrics are densely machine embroidered on a muslin base with the outlines in machine-couched cord. The embroidery is backed with heavy interfacing and then varnished.

▼ **Karen Holt**
Boot
7 × 12 × 4 inches

One of a pair, this machine-embroidered boot is worked on a muslin base, and heavily stitched with metallic threads, scraps of fabric, couched cords, and beads.

◄ Judy Clayton
Embroidered Jewelry
10 × 7 inches

Made in a similar way to the embroidered bowl (page 163), this technique resulted from the search for an embroidery material that is not fragile and is suitable for three-dimensional work.

► Clare Hutchinson
Scheherezade III
5 inches in diameter

This bag, constructed from handmade felt, was an Islamic-inspired pattern worked in embroidery and beads. A plaited silk braid for the strap and a knotted silk tassel with beads make complementary finishing trimmings.

► Jean K. Fryer
"The World is a Stage" Jewelry Box
5 × 4 × 2 inches (closed)

A constructed piece inspired by a love of theater and the desire to create a box which contains an element of surprise. Machine-embroidered silk with applied metallic fabrics and distressed chiffon are laced over cardboard. Dissolvable machine lace is used for the pop-up characters, and a wearable stick-pin completes the effect.

▲ **Janet Haigh**
Pincushions
6 × 6 inches

Stuffed with perfumed
sawdust and stuck with beads
threaded onto pins, these
pincushions incorporate
hand-embroidered sections
with counted cross and long
and short stitch.

▲ **Abigail Mill**
Springtime print tray
9 × 14 inches

A progression of flowerheads
– from bud to full flower and,
thence, to decay and seed
pods – are set in the compart-
ments of the print tray to
create a jewel-like effect.
Machine lace on cold-water-
soluble fabric incorporates
shot silks and velvets, metallic
organzas, and thread.

▲ **Harriet C. Robinson**
Lily Bowls
4 × 4 × 2 inches

Machine embroidery on dissolvable fabric created these small bowls. Each one incorporates small scraps of fabric held in place with plain and metallic threads.

GLOSSARY

Amager embroidery Silk thread work on silk scarves from the Danish island of Amager.

Arraiolos work Portuguese rug embroidery, usually worked in wool on linen.

Ayrshire embroidery A 19th-century whitework technique incorporating surface stitches and needlelace fillings.

Beetlewing embroidery Introduced in the 19th century, this metal thread embroidery originated in southeastern India; used for decorating garments and household articles for the export market.

Berlin woolwork A 19th-century needlepoint technique, usually worked in tent stitch and sometimes including beads.

Carrickmacross lace From the Irish town of that name, fine cotton appliqué on net, stitched to resemble lace.

Casalguidi embroidery Italian whitework consisting of a pulled-work background with raised motifs superimposed on it.

Crivos Portuguese raised whitework embroidery with bullion knots and drawn threads.

Deerfield embroidery Blue and white linen work from New England, similar to crewel embroidery.

Dorset feather stitchery Paisley-type designs built up in feather and buttonhole stitch. Often combined with traditional smocking.

Double-sided embroidery Worked on a vertical frame by two embroiderers, satin stitch is worked in such a way that both sides are the ''right side''.

Filet darning A form of decorating square-mesh net with weaving in cotton or linen.

Hawaiian appliqué A combination of appliqué and quilting with bold designs representing traditional Hawaiian flowers and plants.

Hedebo embroidery Danish drawn thread work of intricate design, combining cutwork and needlelace fillings.

Inlay A type of appliqué in which one fabric is inlaid in another to form a completely flat surface.

Jacobean embroidery Style of crewel embroidery dating from the early 17th century.

Kantha embroidery Quilting from Bangladesh that incorporates color and traditional patterns.

Lacis See filet darning.

Leek embroidery Ecclesiastical embroidery worked on printed fabric.

Levkara Cypriot whitework embroidery similar to Hardanger.

Madeira work Cutwork on fine cotton, often with the addition of appliqué.

Mountmellick work Heavy white cotton embroidery originating in Ireland.

Needlepainting Realistic embroidered pictures, often based on paintings.

Petit point Needlepoint embroidery worked entirely in tent stitch.

Phulkari embroidery Punjabi satin stitch worked in geometric pattrerns.

Ruskin work Linen cutwork popularized by John Ruskin in England's Lake District.

San Blas appliqué Reverse appliqué technique introduced by the Cuna Indians of San Blas, Panama, also known as Mola work.

Soutache embroidery Narrow braid appliqué.

Stained glass appliqué Appliqué resembling stained glass, using bias strips to represent the leadwork.

Tambour work A hooked chain-stitch method often used commercially for applying beads and sequins.

Telemark embroidery Bold floral woolen embroidery from Norway.

Turkeywork Raised pile stitch resembling velvet.

Whitework Any form of white on white embroidery.

INDEX

Acknowledgments

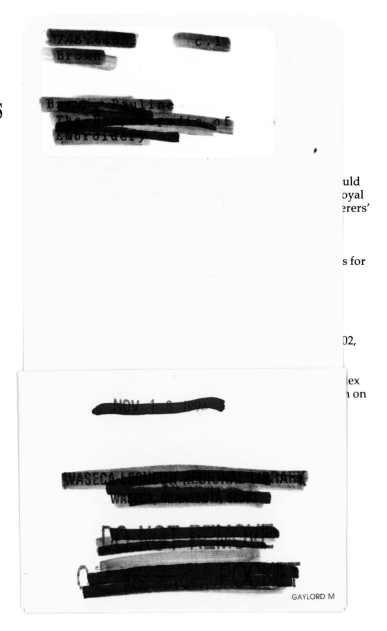

uld
oyal
erers'

s for

02,

lex
n on